THE GREAT CATHOLIC TRIVIA CHALLENGE

Visit our web site at
www.stpauls.us

or call 1-800-343-2522
and request current catalog

The Great Catholic Trivia Challenge

Claire Mary Smith

Editors
William Wayne Stark, Jr., Ph.D.,
Frederick A. Furia, Jr., and Joseph A. Martino, III

ST PAULS

The Scripture citations used in this work are taken from the Catholic Edition of the Revised Standard Version of the Bible (RSV). Catechism excerpts are from the English translation of the Catechism of the Catholic Church, Second Edition, for use in the United States of America, copyright 1994 and 1997.

Nihil Obstat:
Rev. Joseph T. Shenosky, S.T.D.
Censor Librorum

Imprimatur:
✠ Justin Cardinal Rigali
Archbishop of Philadelphia
June 23, 2009

The Nihil Obstat and Imprimatur are official declarations that a book or pamphlet is free of doctrinal or moral error. No implication is contained therein that those who have granted the Nihil Obstat or Imprimatur agree with the contents, opinions, or statements expressed.

Produced and designed in the United States of America by the
Fathers and Brothers of the Society of St. Paul,
2187 Victory Boulevard, Staten Island, New York 10314-6603
as part of their communications apostolate.

ISBN 10: 0-8189-1349-5
ISBN 13: 978-0-8189-1349-5

Printing Information:

Current Printing - first digit	2	3	4	5	6	7	8	9	10

Year of Current Printing - first year shown

2014	2015	2016	2017	2018	2019	2020	2021	2022

Table of Contents

Chapter 1: Beliefs and Practice 1
    Catholic Life 3
    I Confess 5
    Beginnings and Ends 7
    Mass Knowledge 9
    Priestly Questions 11
    Proper Worship 13
    The Ordained Among Us 15
    Catechize Me 17
    Vocabulary 19
    More Vocabulary 21
    Name That Word 25

Chapter 2: Bible 29
    Bible Basics 31
    Old Testament 35
    New Testament 37
    More New Testament 43
    Matthew, Mark, Luke and John 45
    Acts of the Apostles 47
    Numbers to Know 49
    More Old Testament 51
    Still More Old Testament 53
    Prophets are People, Too 55
    The Apostle Quiz 57

Chapter 3: History 59
    North American Connections 61
    Exploration and Discovery 65
    Early Church 69
    More Early Church 73
    American History 75
    Who Am I? 79

Chapter 4: Saints 81
    Coming to America 83
    The Mary Quiz 85
    Our Mother Mary 87
    Gems from St. Augustine 89

Gems from Other Church Fathers 91
More Church Fathers 93
Wonders of Saints 95

Chapter 5: Papacy 99
Papal Challenge 101
John Paul II and Benedict XVI 103
Pope History 105
Popes on the Move 107
Habemus Papam (We Have a Pope) 109
Home of the Holy Father 111

Chapter 6: Science 113
Mathematics, Physics, Astronomy 115
Planets, Moons, Stars and Solar Systems 117
Scientific Discovery 119
Pioneers in Science 121

Chapter 7: Culture 123
Around the World 125
The People Behind the Holidays 129
It's Christmas Time! 131
Art and Architecture 133
Musical Notes 135
Language and Literature 137
Catholic Culture 141
Movie Magic 147
Holy House of Worship 149
Class Acts 153
English Accent 155
Evangelizing the World 157
Connections to Jesus 159
On Guard 161
Traditions of Cultures 163
Nobel Laureates 165
Famous Quotes – Who Said It? 167
Name That College 169
The Acronymous Quiz 171
Take a Guess! 173
Focus on Europe 175
Monks and Hermits 179
Miscellaneous 181
Written Matter 183
Latin American Flavor 185
Catholics of Note 191

Biblical Abbreviations

OLD TESTAMENT

Genesis	Gn	Nehemiah	Ne	Baruch	Ba
Exodus	Ex	Tobit	Tb	Ezekiel	Ezk
Leviticus	Lv	Judith	Jdt	Daniel	Dn
Numbers	Nb	Esther	Est	Hosea	Ho
Deuteronomy	Dt	1 Maccabees	1 M	Joel	Jl
Joshua	Jos	2 Maccabees	2 M	Amos	Am
Judges	Jg	Job	Jb	Obadiah	Ob
Ruth	Rt	Psalms	Ps	Jonah	Jon
1 Samuel	1 S	Proverbs	Pr	Micah	Mi
2 Samuel	2 S	Ecclesiastes	Ec	Nahum	Na
1 Kings	1 K	Song of Songs	Sg	Habakkuk	Hab
2 Kings	2 K	Wisdom	Ws	Zephaniah	Zp
1 Chronicles	1 Ch	Sirach	Si	Haggai	Hg
2 Chronicles	2 Ch	Isaiah	Is	Malachi	Ml
Ezra	Ezr	Jeremiah	Jr	Zechariah	Zc
		Lamentations	Lm		

NEW TESTAMENT

Matthew	Mt	Ephesians	Eph	Hebrews	Heb
Mark	Mk	Philippians	Ph	James	Jm
Luke	Lk	Colossians	Col	1 Peter	1 P
John	Jn	1 Thessalonians	1 Th	2 Peter	2 P
Acts	Ac	2 Thessalonians	2 Th	1 John	1 Jn
Romans	Rm	1 Timothy	1 Tm	2 John	2 Jn
1 Corinthians	1 Cor	2 Timothy	2 Tm	3 John	3 Jn
2 Corinthians	2 Cor	Titus	Tt	Jude	Jude
Galatians	Gal	Philemon	Phm	Revelation	Rv

Chapter One
Beliefs and Practice

Q1: What is "the source and summit of Christian life," according to the Second Vatican Council?
   a. Family
   b. Education
   c. The Eucharist
   d. Prayer
   e. Ecumenism

Q2: What do we celebrate on the Feast of Corpus Christi?
   a. The precious wounds on Christ's Body
   b. The institution of the Eucharist
   c. The bodily Resurrection of Christ
   d. The sign of the cross
   e. The passion of Christ

Q3: By which name is the festive holiday – Shrove Tuesday – better known?
   a. Beethoven's birthday
   b. Purim
   c. Epiphany
   d. Mardi Gras
   e. Maundy Thursday

A1: (c) The Eucharist (*Dogmatic Constitution on the Church*, no. 11).

A2: (b) The institution of the Eucharist at the Last Supper, including the Real Presence of the Lord's Body and Blood at Mass. "Corpus Christi" is Latin for "Body of Christ." Pope Urban IV instituted the feast in 1264 and asked St. Thomas Aquinas to write a special liturgy for it.

A3: (d) Mardi Gras or Fat Tuesday marks the last day before Lent – the period of prayer, fasting and almsgiving before Easter. The pre-Lent season is known as Carnival and is popular in Rio de Janeiro, New Orleans, Venice, and elsewhere.

Q4: What is the proper punishment for a priest guilty of a direct violation of the seal of Confession?
    a. Public shunning
    b. Gentle warning
    c. Excommunication
    d. Inquisition
    e. Death penalty

Q5: According to St. Augustine, Baptism, prayer and penance are three ways in which _____.
    a. We can demonstrate our faith
    b. We can evangelize
    c. We can show an example for others
    d. Sins are forgiven
    e. We can feel better

Q6: What must one do before setting foot in the Confessional (besides sin)?
    a. Say the Hail Mary
    b. Beat one's breast
    c. Rehearse sins in front of friends
    d. Examine one's conscience
    e. Sprinkle one's self with holy water

A4: (c) Excommunication. A priest who directly violates the seal of confession incurs excommunication. A priest who indirectly violates the seal "is to be punished in accord with the seriousness of the offense," according to Canon Law.

A5: (d) Sins are forgiven (Source: *Sermon to Catechumens on the Creed*, 388 A.D.).

A6: (d) Conduct a prayerful examination of conscience.

Q7: Biblically, it appears that some people will not have to die. Which people?
    a. The people alive on earth at the time of the Second Coming
    b. The people alive on earth in the year 2500
    c. Certain future popes
    d. Certain future kings
    e. People from other planets

Q8: Which *three* sacraments should Catholics seek on their deathbed?
    a. Holy Orders
    b. Confession
    c. Holy Communion
    d. Anointing of the Sick
    e. A second Baptism

Q9: What does the water of Baptism wash away from a person's soul?
    a. Original sin
    b. Personal sin
    c. Venial sin
    d. Mortal sin
    e. All of the above

Q10: Where would the souls of Noah and his wife have gone after they died?
    a. Heaven
    b. Limbo
    c. Purgatory
    d. Abraham's Bosom
    e. Noah's Ark

A7: (a) The people alive on earth at the time of the Second Coming will be taken alive, body and soul, to the state of their eternal destiny.

A8: (b, c and d) Confession (Jn 20:23), Holy Communion (Jn 6:53), and the Anointing of the Sick (Jm 5:14-15; Mk 6:12-13). A second Baptism is not possible. Our final Communion that we receive shortly before death is called "Viaticum" because we need it on our way to eternity. "Via" means way.

A9: (e) All of the above (*Catechism of the Catholic Church* #1263). However, a newborn's soul would only have original sin.

A10: (d) Abraham's Bosom. The saintly people of Old Testament times could not go to heaven before the Resurrection of Jesus Christ. The dead had to wait for the Messiah in a place known as Abraham's Bosom, Sheol, or Hades (See Lk 16:22-23 and *Catechism of the Catholic Church* #633).

Q11: In the United States, what should we do just before receiving Communion at a Mass?
  a. Genuflect
  b. Kneel
  c. Bow our head
  d. Shut our eyes
  e. Nothing

Q12: According to the Second Vatican Council, which musical instrument should be held in high esteem at Mass?
  a. Harp
  b. Trumpet
  c. Violin
  d. Pipe organ
  e. Flute

Q13: How many Bible readings are there at Sunday Mass?
  a. Zero
  b. One
  c. Two
  d. Three or more
  e. Whatever Protestants have plus ten

Q14: What type of sacred music takes a place of pride in the Roman liturgy?
  a. Operatic
  b. Soprano
  c. Baritone
  d. Gregorian Chant
  e. Baroque

A11: (c) Bow our head. This gesture is stipulated by the U.S. Conference of Catholic Bishops' adaptations to the General Instruction of the Roman Missal (GIRM 160) for Masses celebrated in the Roman Rite.

A12: (d) The pipe organ. The Second Vatican Council document, *Constitution on the Sacred Liturgy* (no. 120), states that in the Latin Church the pipe organ "is to be held in high esteem" and "powerfully lifts up man's mind to God."

A13: (d) Three or more, usually one reading from the Old Testament (Hebrew Scriptures), one from the New Testament other than the Gospel, and one Gospel reading.

A14: (d) Gregorian Chant, as recommended by the General Instruction of the Roman Missal.

Q15: What color do priests wear on Palm Sunday?
    a. Green
    b. Pink
    c. Purple
    d. White
    e. Red

Q16: What is the most common color of the vestments that priests wear for Mass?
    a. Green
    b. Pink
    c. Purple
    d. White
    e. Red

Q17: What color vestment would be used for a funeral Mass of a pope?
    a. Green
    b. Pink
    c. Purple
    d. White
    e. Red

Q18: What prayer must priests say every day no matter where they are?
    a. Rosary
    b. Divine Mercy chaplet
    c. Novena
    d. The Divine Office
    e. Kaddish

Q19: Which *two* parts of the body are generally anointed with oil by a priest as part of the Sacrament of Anointing of the Sick (formerly called the Sacrament of Extreme Unction)?
    a. Hands
    b. Feet
    c. Ankles
    d. Forehead
    e. Neck

A15: (e) Red. Priests wear red vestments on Palm Sunday, Good Friday, Pentecost Sunday and the feast days of martyrs. Red symbolizes blood and fire.

A16: (a) Green. Denoting nature and eternal life, green is worn in Ordinary Time. White, for purity and light, is worn in the Christmas and Easter seasons. Violet vestments, signifying sorrow and penance, are worn during Advent and Lent.

A17: (e) Red.

A18: (d) The Divine Office. These compilations of prayers and readings, which are said at different parts of the day, are also called the Breviary or the Liturgy of the Hours. The Church also encourages lay men and women to say these official prayers for the salvation of the world. Deacons must say parts of the Divine Office as well.

A19: (a, d) The forehead and hands.

Q20: What is the correct posture of the faithful at Mass during Scripture readings prior to the Gospel?
  a. Sitting
  b. Standing
  c. Kneeling
  d. Walking
  e. Liturgical Dancing

Q21: What is the correct posture of the faithful at Mass during the Gospel?
  a. Sitting
  b. Standing
  c. Kneeling
  d. Walking
  e. Liturgical Dancing

Q22: What is the correct posture of the faithful at Mass during the consecration?
  a. Sitting
  b. Standing
  c. Kneeling
  d. Walking
  e. Liturgical Dancing

Q23: The U.S. bishops encourage the presence of all of the following at a Roman Rite Mass except for _____.
  a. Immovable altar
  b. Flowers and candles
  c. Relics of martyrs
  d. Visible crucifix
  e. Multitudes of lay people distributing Communion

Q24: Which of these Christian groups is most similar to Catholics in doctrine and worship?
  a. Anglicans
  b. Methodists
  c. Greek Orthodox
  d. Lutherans
  e. Baptists

A20: (a) Sitting.

A21: (b) Standing.

A22: (c) Kneeling. These guidelines are covered in No. 43 of the 2002 General Instruction of the Roman Missal.

A23: (e) Multitudes of lay people distributing Holy Communion. The *ordinary ministers* of Holy Communion are bishops, priests and deacons, whose sacramental ordination uniquely configures them to ministry at the altar. However, lay people may serve as *extraordinary ministers* of Holy Communion if the congregation is unusually large.

A24: (c) Greek Orthodox (and other Orthodox Christians, such as Russian Orthodox). Theses Churches possess all seven Sacraments, a valid priesthood, and the Sacrifice of the Mass since they have maintained apostolic succession.

Q25: From lowest to highest, what are the three ordained ministries of the Sacrament of Holy Orders?

    a. Deacon, priest, bishop   d. Bishop, cardinal, pope

    b. Priest, deacon, bishop   e. Brother, friar, monk

    c. Lector, priest, bishop

Q26: Who is the original and ordinary minister of Confirmation?

    a. The deacon   d. The altar boy

    b. The priest   e. The CCD teacher

    c. The bishop

Q27: Who may administer Baptism to you?

    a. A deacon   d. In an emergency, anybody

    b. A priest   e. All of the above

    c. A bishop

Q28: The pope teaches infallibly when he speaks ex-cathedra, which literally is Latin for:

    a. Extemporaneously   d. Outdoors

    b. From the Chair   e. Holding a Bible

    c. In a cathedral

Q29: After a pope canonizes a person as a saint, we can be confident that _____.

    a. The person is in heaven

    b. The person never sinned

    c. The person's body already rose

    d. The person is now an angel

    e. The person will appear in a vision to a worthy person

Q30: What step must precede the canonization of a saint?

    a. Tribunal   d. Excommunication

    b. Beatification   e. Exorcism

    c. Rite of Initiation

Q31: Which individuals make a promise of celibacy and obedience, but generally do not make a vow of poverty?

    a. Friars

    b. Nuns

    c. Franciscan, Dominican, Augustinian and Jesuit priests

    d. Lay people

    e. Diocesan priests

A25: (a) Deacon, priest, bishop.

A26: (c) The bishop is the original and ordinary minister of Confirmation. However, a bishop may delegate this authority to a priest. In the East, priests often baptize and confirm babies on the same day.

A27: (e) All of the above.

A28: (b) "From the Chair" (of Peter) or by a special exercise of the pope's teaching office. God prevents the pope from teaching error when making extraordinary declarations of a teaching on faith and morals in his capacity as the official teacher of Christian doctrine thanks to the promises of divine assistance that Jesus made to St. Peter. This is known as infallibility.

A29: (a) The person is in heaven. Therefore, we can be confident that our prayerful requests for the saint's intercession will be heard.

A30: (b) Beatification.

A31: (e) Diocesan priests. Monks, friars, nuns and priests of religious orders make at least three vows (poverty, chastity and obedience), sometimes four or five. Although diocesan priests do not make vows of poverty, "clerics are to foster simplicity of life and are to refrain from all things that have a semblance of vanity," according to Canon 282 of the Code of Canon Law.

Q32: According to Catholic teaching, salvation is by _____.
    a. Grace   d. Confidence
    b. Belief   e. Enlightenment
    c. Works

Q33: What does CCD stand for?
    a. Confraternity of Christian Doctrine
    b. Catholic Christian Discipline
    c. Communion, Confirmation and Doctrines
    d. Co-Ed Church Drama
    e. Calling Catholic Delinquents

Q34: Which *three* conditions must be met for a mortal sin to exist?
    a. It was a grave matter
    b. Someone was hurt
    c. The act was intentional
    d. There was full knowledge and consent
    e. It was committed by a Catholic

Q35: What type of sin are babies born with?
    a. Venial   d. Original
    b. Mortal   e. Illegal
    c. Personal

Q36: Which prayer came to us straight from the mouth of Jesus?
    a. Hail Mary   d. Nicene Creed
    b. Our Father   e. Act of Contrition
    c. Glory Be

Q37: On which day of the year would Mass not be celebrated in Catholic churches?
    a. Christmas Eve   d. Thanksgiving
    b. Halloween   e. Labor Day
    c. Good Friday

A32: (a) Grace. In the *Catechism of the Catholic Church*, see sections 1987 to 2029 on grace and justification.

A33: (a) Confraternity of Christian Doctrine.

A34: (a, c, d) To qualify as a mortal sin, the action must constitute a grave matter, and must have been done intentionally and with full consent and knowledge of the seriousness of the sin.

A35: (d) Original sin. This sin, which we all inherited from Adam and Eve, is wiped away in Baptism.

A36: (b) The words of the Our Father (or "Lord's Prayer") were given to us by Jesus and were recorded in the Bible (Lk 11:2-4 and Mt 6:9-13).

A37: (c) Good Friday. This solemn day commemorates the crucifixion and death of our Lord.

Q38: What word refers to the supernatural gift of God's life to the souls of human beings for our eternal salvation?

    a. Hyperdulia

    b. Virtue

    c. Grace

    d. Mysticism

    e. Fellowship

Q39: What theological word refers to the transformation of one's soul that brings a person into friendship with God from his previous state of enmity with God?

    a. Metamorphosis

    b. Justification

    c. Transmutation

    d. Renewal

    e. Fraternization

Q40: What word refers to the practice of Christian asceticism with the intent to overcome sin, slay the desires of the flesh, strengthen the will, and progress in virtue?

    a. Epicureanism

    b. Gastronomy

    c. Sensuality

    d. Mortification

    e. Backsliding

Q41: What word refers to a bishop's official church in which he presides, teaches, and conducts worship for the Christian community?

    a. Basilica

    b. Oratory

    c. Bethel

    d. Chancery

    e. Cathedral

Q42: What are the underground chambers in Rome called where many early Christians were buried?

    a. Cloisters

    b. Caves

    c. Labyrinths

    d. Catacombs

    e. Dungeons

A38: Grace. Those who possess sanctifying grace are truly children of God. Human beings come into the world without sanctifying grace.

A39: (b) Justification. It occurs when a person receives an infusion of God's grace into his soul; thus, he is born to a new life as a member of the Body of Christ. See the *Catechism of the Catholic Church* (especially ## 402, 617, 654, 1266, 1446 and 1987-2001).

A40: (d) Mortification. This practice – intended to train the soul for virtuous living and deemed pleasing to God when the person is in a state of grace – can include penances, hardships, austerities or sacrificial charitable endeavors.

A41: (e) Cathedral. This chief church of a diocese is where a bishop has his chair (cathedra), a symbolic term representing his authority to govern his diocese.

A42: (d) Catacombs. Dug between the second and early fifth centuries, these man-made underground maze-like passageways served as cemeteries, especially for Christians. "During the persecutions, especially in the time of Pope Saint Damasus (366-384), the catacombs became real shrines of the martyrs, centers of devotion and of pilgrimage for Christians from every part of the empire" (www.catacombe.roma.it/en/intro.html).

Q43: What word refers to the teaching authority of the Church?
    a. Decalogue   d. Motu Propio
    b. Filioque   e. Synod
    c. Magisterium

Q44: What term refers to the fact that after the consecration at Mass, the Lord Jesus is truly there, Body, Blood, Soul and Divinity?
    a. Tabernacle   d. Real Presence
    b. Dirge   e. Prelate
    c. Hyperdulia

Q45: What word refers to the vessel for holding small Hosts to be distributed at Communion?
    a. Ciborium   d. Antiphon
    b. Scapular   e. Sabachthani
    c. Requiem

Q46: What word refers to an authoritatively stated truth pertaining to faith or morals, revealed by God, transmitted by the Apostles, and proclaimed by the Church to be believed by all the faithful?
    a. Decalogue   d. Synod
    b. Dogma   e. Reformation
    c. Papal bull

Q47: What word refers to the science of explaining and defending religious doctrines?
    a. Apologetics   d. Donatism
    b. Scholasticism   e. Explication
    c. Sabbatarianism

Q48: What word refers to a total defection from the Christian religion after previous acceptance?
    a. Exorcism   d. Apostasy
    b. Prelate   e. Hyperdulia
    c. Desecration

Q49: What word refers to the head or superior of a community of monks?
    a. Principal   d. Pontiff
    b. Abbot   e. Magister
    c. Executor

A43: (c) Magisterium. The Magisterium consists of the Catholic bishops of the world teaching in union with the pope. The Catholic Church received this office of teaching from Christ, who said, "Go therefore and make disciples of all nations, baptizing them in the name of the Father and of the Son and of the Holy Spirit, teaching them to observe all that I have commanded you; and lo, I am with you always, to the close of the age" (Mt 28:19-20).

A44: (d) Real Presence. The belief is based in part on the sixth chapter of the Gospel of John, in which Jesus said, "...he who eats my flesh and drinks my blood has eternal life, and I will raise him up at the last day. For my flesh is food indeed, and my blood is drink indeed. He who eats my flesh and drinks my blood abides in me, and I in him" (Jn 6:54-56).

A45: (a) Ciborium. This round-shaped vessel resembles a chalice and is usually made of gold or silver.

A46: (b) Dogma. A dogma is a revealed truth, defined by the Church, to be believed by all the faithful. All dogmas are doctrines, but not all doctrines are dogmas.

A47: (a) Apologetics.

A48: (d) Apostasy.

A49: (b) Abbot.

Q50: What word is the gold- or silver-plated vessel that carries the Eucharist Host when the Blessed Sacrament is exposed for Eucharistic adoration?
  a. Sanctuary
  b. Monstrance
  c. Reliquary
  d. Antechamber
  e. Humidor

Q51: What word is a synonym for hermit or a person who goes to live in the desert or other secluded place to seek God in solitude?
  a. Socialite
  b. Debutante
  c. Patrician
  d. Anchorite
  e. Bird of Minerva

A50: (b) Monstrance.

A51: (d) Anchorite. In the Old Testament, the prophet Elijah is a precursor to the hermetic life of future ascetics such as John the Baptist and St. Anthony of Egypt.

Q52: Name the marriage preparation course that Catholics take prior to their wedding.
- a. Decalogue
- b. Pre-Cana
- c. RCIA
- d. CCD
- e. Bible study

Q53: What word refers to official letters from the pope, usually regarding doctrine?
- a. Homily
- b. Encyclical
- c. Synod
- d. Requiem
- e. Exegesis

Q54: What word describes the process of purification or purging that souls of heaven-bound individuals go through after death if they die in God's friendship and grace but are not yet holy enough to behold the face of God?
- a. Penance
- b. Regeneration
- c. Justification
- d. Purgatory
- e. Canonization

Q55: What word refers to the remission of temporal punishment for already forgiven sins?
- a. Decastigation
- b. Indulgence
- c. Confession
- d. Laicization
- e. Justification

Q56: Originating from an Italian word for "pumpkin," what word refers to a small skullcap worn by a cardinal?
- a. Turban
- b. Diadem
- c. Zucchetto
- d. Wimple
- e. Stetson

Q57: Meaning "without shoes," what word refers to religious orders whose members go barefoot or wear sandals?
- a. Discalced
- b. Cloistered
- c. Consecrated
- d. Reformed
- e. Novitiate

Q58: What word refers to nine days of prayer?
- a. Motu Proprio
- b. Marathon
- c. Novena
- d. Retreat
- e. Benediction

A52: (b) Pre-Cana, named after the wedding feast at Cana in Galilee (Jn 2:1-12), where Jesus turned water into wine.

A53: (b) Encyclical. Encyclicals are addressed to the world's bishops and sometimes to the entire Catholic faithful.

A54: (d) Purgatory.

A55: (b) Indulgence. A person in the state of grace may obtain an indulgence for himself or for a deceased person in purgatory by piously performing specific good works or prayers issued by the Church. A list of available indulgences is available online at www.ourladyswarriors.org/indulge/plenary.htm.

A56: (c) Zucchetto. In Italian, "zucca" means "pumpkin" and also humorously refers to someone's head. The pope wears a white zucchetto, a cardinal wears a scarlet one, and a bishop wears a purple one.

A57: (a) Discalced.

A58: (c) Novena.

Q59: Also known as the Song of Mary, what refers to the prayer voiced by the Blessed Mother when she visited Elizabeth, shortly after the Angel Gabriel told Mary she would become the Lord's mother?
- a. Kaddish
- b. Magnificat
- c. Invocation
- d. Litany
- e. Adoration

Q60: What word calls to mind these words of the Gospel of John: "The Word was made Flesh" (Jn 1:14)?
- a. Incarnation
- b. Ascension
- c. Presentation
- d. Gethsemane
- e. Epiphany

Q61: What word is a process by which God enriches the soul and makes it holy?
- a. Sanctification
- b. Laicization
- c. Desecration
- d. Relativism
- e. Beatification

Q62: Which is an outward sign instituted by Christ to give grace?
- a. Sacrament
- b. Sackcloth
- c. Synod
- d. Psalm
- e. Novena

Q63: What book did Pope John Paul II call "a sure norm for teaching the faith" and "a sure and authentic reference text for teaching Catholic doctrine"?
- a. *Left to Tell* by Immaculée Ilibagiza
- b. *Reason to Believe* by Ron Tesoriero
- c. *Heaven is for Real* by Todd Burpo
- d. *Story of a Soul* by St. Thérèse of Lisieux
- e. The *Catechism of the Catholic Church*

Q64: What word refers to Pope Benedict XVI's brief, concise summary of the *Catechism of the Catholic Church*?
- a. Antiphon
- b. Compendium
- c. Imprimatur
- d. Abstract
- e. Manual

A59: (b) Magnificat.

A60: (a) Incarnation.

A61: (a) Sanctification.

A62: (a) Sacrament. The seven Sacraments are Baptism, Holy Communion, Confirmation, Confession, Marriage, Holy Orders and the Anointing of the Sick.

A63: (e) The *Catechism of the Catholic Church.*

A64: (b) Compendium. Both the *Compendium* and the full-length *Catechism of the Catholic Church* can be purchased at bookstores or read in full on the Internet.

Chapter Two
Bible

Q65: What are the two divisions of the Christian Bible?
    a. Papyrus and Scrolls
    b. Torah and Talmud
    c. Epistles and Acts
    d. Latin and Italian
    e. Old Testament and New Testament

Q66: What is the New Testament?
    a. An Arabic text delivered to the prophet Muhammad by the angel
       Gabriel in the early 7th century
    b. Sacred writings delivered to Joseph Smith, Jr., by the angel Moroni in
       1830
    c. Compiled hymns, incantations, and rituals from ancient India
    d. Sermons of Gautama Buddha
    e. The second part of the Christian Bible, written in the first century,
       originally in Greek

Q67: How many books make up the New Testament?
    a. 4
    b. 7
    c. 17
    d. 27
    e. 103

Q68: How many books make up the Old Testament?
    a. 4
    b. 6
    c. 46
    d. 64
    e. 446

Q69: Which of the following Apostles did *not* write any books of the New
Testament?
    a. St. Peter
    b. St. John
    c. St. Jude
    d. St. Paul
    e. St. Thomas

A65: (e) Old Testament and New Testament.

A66: (e) Choice "a" refers to the Koran, choice "b" refers to the Book of Mormon, choice "c" refers to sacred Hindu texts known as the Vedas, and choice "d" refers to the sūtras of Buddhism.

A67: (d) 27.

A68: (c) 46.

A69: (e) St. Thomas did not write Scripture. Overall, only five members of the original Twelve Apostles (Matthew, John, James, Peter, Jude) contributed writings that would become part of the Bible. Although not one of the original Apostles, St. Paul also wrote Scripture, 13 epistles in all. St. Mark and St. Luke, neither of whom was an Apostle, each wrote a Gospel.

Q70: What is the Old Testament?
   a. A rough draft of the New Testament
   b. The diary of Adam and Eve
   c. The teachings of Buddha, written in Pali, Sanskrit and Tibetan
   d. Writings of angels
   e. The first part of the Christian Bible, originally written in Hebrew, featuring God's covenant with Abraham and the revelation of Himself to the people of Israel

Q71: In the New Testament, Jesus often speaks in _____, which are stories, generally fictional, that teach a moral truth.
   a. Riddles
   b. Tongues
   c. Fables
   d. Parables
   e. Myths

Q72: Which of the following was not a parable told by Jesus?
   a. Parable of the Good Samaritan (Lk 10:30-37)
   b. Parable of the Lost Coin (Lk 15:8-10)
   c. Parable of the Rich Fool (Lk 12:16-21)
   d. Parable of the Lost Sheep (Lk 15:3-7; Mt 18:10-14)
   e. Parable of the Dog in the Manger (Jn 6:72-76)

A70: (e).

A71: (d) Parables.

A72: (e) This was not a parable but rather one of Aesop's fables. The noncanonical Gospel According to Thomas has Jesus refer to it.

Q73: According to the Book of Judges, what was the only way to deprive Samson of his superhuman strength?
    a. Tickle him
    b. Strip him
    c. Cut his hair
    d. Say a magic word
    e. Remove his ring of power

Q74: In the Book of Samuel, what is the famous line that the boy Samuel says three times to Eli?
    a. "Where is Delila?"
    b. "Here I am, for you called me"
    c. "Seek and you shall find"
    d. "Peace be with you"
    e. "Sam I am."

Q75: The Gospel of Luke contains the warning, "Remember Lot's wife" (Lk 17:32). What happened to Lot's wife?
    a. She was swallowed by a whale
    b. She was swallowed into the ground
    c. She was captured by the Philistines
    d. She was struck by lightning
    e. She was turned into a pillar of salt

Q76: All of the following sayings come from the New Testament except for one. Which does not?
    a. "Physician, heal thyself" (Lk 10:17)
    b. "The truth will set you free" (Jn 8:32)
    c. "To err is human, to repent divine" (Jn 22:6)
    d. "A house divided against itself cannot stand" (Mk 3:25)
    e. "No one can serve two masters" (Mt 6:24)

Q77: All of the following expressions are rooted in the Old Testament except for one. Which is not?
    a. "Am I my brother's keeper?" (Gn 4:9)
    b. "Eat to live, and not live to eat" (Pr 32:2)
    c. "I have escaped by the skin of my teeth" (Jb 19:20)
    d. "The apple of his eye" (Zc 2:8)
    e. "There is nothing new under the sun" (Ec 1:9)

A73: (c) Cut off his long hair. An angel told the parents of Samson that they would have a baby son who would deliver Israel from the hand of the Philistines. The angel also warned them, "No razor shall come upon his head, for the boy shall be a Nazarite to God from birth" (Jg 13:5). Samson was the last of the Judges of Israel.

A74: (b) Each time that Samuel heard his name being called, he reported to Eli, but Eli replied that he had not called him. Eli, a judge and high-priest, finally realized it was the Lord calling Samuel and told the boy: "Go, lie down; and if he calls you, you shall say, 'Speak, Lord, for your servant is listening.'"

A75: (e) She turned into a pillar of salt (Gn 19:24-26). Despite a warning from angels to flee without looking back, Lot's wife looked back at the sinful cities of Sodom and Gomorrah as they were destroyed by brimstone and fire from the Lord.

A76: (c) This quotation comes to us from Benjamin Franklin (1706-1790), as recorded in his *Poor Richard's Almanac* (1732).

A77: (b) This one is also from Ben Franklin's 1732 *Poor Richard's Almanac*.

Q78: Which of the four Gospels is not like the others?
  a. Matthew
  b. Mark
  c. Luke
  d. John

Q79: What single word belongs in all three blanks: "In the beginning was the
_____, and the _____ was with God, and the _____ was God."
  a. Law   d. Bible
  b. Word   e. End
  c. Creation

Q80: The author of the last book of the New Testament, known as the Book
of Revelation or Apocalypse, identifies himself as:
  a. John
  b. The Elder
  c. The Prophet
  d. Andrew
  e. The Omega

Q81: The Book of Revelation contains a statement addressing the "seven
churches of Asia" (Rv 1:4). The seven churches are located in Ephesus,
Smyrna, Pergamum, Thyatira, Sardis, Laodicea and _____.
  a. Antioch
  b. Jerusalem
  c. Philadelphia
  d. Nazareth
  e. Babylon

Q82: Which Apostle, known as the "Apostle to the Gentiles," presumably
never met Jesus before the Crucifixion and Resurrection?
  a. St. Paul
  b. St. James
  c. St. Thomas
  d. St. Simon
  e. St. Bartholomew

A78: (d) John. The first three Gospels – Matthew, Mark and Luke – are known as the synoptic Gospels because they run roughly parallel to the others, recounting many of the same stories, often in the same order. The Gospel of John contains some of the same information but is more distinct in the material chosen, placing greater emphasis on the words and discourses of Jesus.

A79: (b) Word. The quotation is the first sentence of the Gospel of John.

A80: (a) John. Church Fathers such as St. Justin Martyr, St. Irenaeus, and St. Clement of Alexandria identified the author as St. John the Apostle, but other early Fathers, including Eusebius of Caesarea and St. Cyril of Jerusalem, denied his authorship. One proposed idea is that the author was a disciple of St. John the Apostle.

A81: (c) This Philadelphia was located in present-day Turkey.

A82: (a) St. Paul, who was not one of the original Twelve Apostles. St. Paul was on his way to Damascus to persecute Christians after the Resurrection when he encountered a light "brighter than the sun" (Ac 26:13) and a voice admonishing him, "Saul, Saul, why do you persecute me?" (Ac 26:14). Jesus revealed Himself to Paul and gave him his mission of delivering His message of salvation to the Gentiles.

Q83: The Mosaic Law of the Old Testament was imposed upon the Jews before Christ's time. Which of the following is *not* an example of Mosaic Law?
   a. Circumcision
   b. Abstaining from pig or camel meat and from fish without fins and scales
   c. Women being ritually unclean after childbirth
   d. Sacrificing animals without blemish
   e. Worshipping God on Sundays

Q84: What word refers to the first five books of the Old Testament (Genesis, Exodus, Leviticus, Numbers, and Deuteronomy)?
   a. Pentateuch
   b. Talmud
   c. Il Cinque
   d. Targum
   e. Septuagint

Q85: Which of the following is *not* one of the Ten Plagues sent by God to punish Egypt for the Pharaoh's refusal to grant Moses' request to free the Israelites from slavery in Egypt?
   a. Unhealable boils
   b. River water turning to blood
   c. Killer bees
   d. Darkness
   e. Death of every firstborn male in the land of Egypt

Q86: Which of the following is *not* a way in which Moses was helped when he led about 600,000 Israelite men and their families out of Egypt and toward the Promised Land?
   a. He was led by God, in the form of a pillar of cloud in the day and pillar of fire by night (Ex 13:21-22)
   b. The parting of the Red Sea, allowing Israelites to walk on dry land when the Egyptians were chasing them (Ex 14:21-23)
   c. God sent quail and manna from the sky to the hungry Israelites (Ex 16:13-16)
   d. Water was miraculously drawn from a rock (Ex 17:6)
   e. A golden calf miraculously led the people through a mountain

A83: (e) Worshipping God on Sundays. In Apostolic times, Sunday became the day of solemn worship for Christians instead of the Jewish Sabbath, which lasted from Friday evening to Saturday evening.

A84: (a) Pentateuch (or Torah).

A85: (c) Killer bees. An account of the Ten Plagues appears in the Book of Exodus, Chapters 7 to 11. After the Tenth Plague – the death of every first-born male in the land of Egypt – was unleashed, Pharaoh not only allowed the Israelites to go, but *commanded* that they leave.

A86: (e) The golden calf mentioned in Exodus was built by Aaron, the brother of Moses, during the 40 days and nights that Moses was atop Mount Sinai getting the Ten Commandments. The Israelites, fearful that Moses would not return, asked Aaron to make the calf as a god to be worshipped. God punished this evil deed by sending disease (Ex 32:35).

Q87: In the Book of Exodus, God appears to Moses and says, "I am the God of your father, the God of _____, the God of _____, and the God of _____" (Ex 3:6).
- a. Men, Women, Angels
- b. Adam, Noah, Joseph
- c. Abraham, Isaac, Jacob
- d. Samuel, David, Solomon
- e. The Father, the Son, the Holy Spirit

Q88: Which of the following is *not* true about Abraham?
- a. God made an everlasting covenant with him and promised he would be the ancestor of many nations
- b. God promised the land of Canaan to his descendants
- c. God told him the sign of the covenant would be that baby boys, from then on, would have to be circumcised
- d. God promised that his 90-year-old childless wife, Sarah, would bear a son, to be named Isaac
- e. God promised that the covenant would be established through his son Ishmael

Q89: Which Old Testament figure, renamed "Israel" by God, was the father of twelve sons and the ancestor of the Twelve Tribes of Israel?
- a. Joseph
- b. Jacob
- c. Noah
- d. Solomon
- e. Ishmael

Q90: Name the temple builder of the Old Testament whose parents were King David and the beautiful Bathsheba.
- a. Goliath
- b. Solomon
- c. Ahab
- d. Moses
- e. Aaron

A87: (c) Abraham, Isaac and Jacob. Abraham was the father of Isaac, grandfather of Jacob, and great-grandfather of Joseph. God also identified Himself to Moses as "I Am Who Am" (Ex 3:14).

A88: (e) The covenant would be established through Abraham's son Isaac, not Ishmael.

A89: (b) Jacob.

A90: (b) Solomon.

Q91: Which of the following is *not* a book in the New Testament?
  a. Titus
  b. Philemon
  c. Joshua
  d. Hebrews
  e. Jude

Q92: Which Apostle was told by Jesus: "I will give you the keys to the kingdom of heaven. Whatever you bind on earth shall be bound in heaven; and whatever you loose on earth shall be loosed in heaven" (Mt 16:19)?
  a. St. Paul
  b. St. James
  c. St. Philip
  d. St. John
  e. St. Peter

Q93: What are the most famous four words said by Jesus at the Last Supper?
  a. "My work is done"
  b. "Peace be with you"
  c. "Get up and walk"
  d. "This is my body"
  e. "Forgive us our trespasses"

A91: (c) Joshua. The Book of Joshua follows Deuteronomy in the Old Testament. Hebrews, Titus, Philemon and Jude are all in the New Testament. In all, there are 27 books of the New Testament and 46 books in the Old Testament (the Bibles commonly used by Protestants have 39 Old Testament books – you get bonus points if you know which books make up the difference).

A92: (e) St. Peter. Jesus said to him: "You are Peter, and upon this rock I will build my church, and the gates of the netherworld shall not prevail against it. I will give you the keys to the kingdom of heaven. Whatever you bind on earth shall be bound in heaven; and whatever you loose on earth shall be loosed in heaven" (Mt 16:17-19).

A93: (d) "This is my body" (Mt 26:26). Thus, Jesus instituted the Eucharist.

Q94: After Jesus was baptized in the Jordan River by John the Baptist, the Spirit of God was seen coming down in the form of what?
    a. Fire
    b. Wind
    c. A dove
    d. A lamb
    e. A cloud

Q95: What did Jesus say about the angels of children?
    a. They are small
    b. They are purer than snow
    c. They behold the face of God the Father
    d. Children can see them
    e. They have names

Q96: As punishment for not believing the Angel Gabriel that his wife would bear a son in her old age, Zechariah was made unable to _____.
    a. Walk
    b. Speak
    c. Eat
    d. Work
    e. Sleep

Q97: After Zacchaeus, the tax collector, came down from the sycamore tree, what did he tell Jesus he would give to the poor?
    a. His house
    b. Fruit from his tree
    c. His shoes
    d. Half of his belongings
    e. His gold and silver

Q98: How long had Lazarus been buried when Jesus raised him from the dead?
    a. Three hours
    b. One day
    c. Two days
    d. Four days
    e. A week

Q99: In the Gospel of Matthew, Jesus recommends doing what *three* things in private in order to avoid receiving human praise?
    a. Praying
    b. Fasting
    c. Helping the needy
    d. Reading
    e. Artwork

Q100: In the Gospel of Luke, which person calls out from the netherworld, in torment?
    a. A rich man who feasted sumptuously daily
    b. A poor man with sores
    c. A brother of the Prodigal Son
    d. A long-time prostitute
    e. Jezebel

Q101: In the Gospel of Matthew, Jesus instructs us not to waste our time worrying about what *three* things?
    a. Friendships
    b. Food
    c. Drink
    d. Clothing
    e. The past

A94: (c) Dove (Mt 3:16).

A95: (c) Their angels "always behold the face of my Father who is in heaven" (Mt 18:11).

A96: (b) He was unable to speak until the promise came true (Lk 1:20). Zechariah and Elizabeth became the parents of St. John the Baptist.

A97: (d) Half of his belongings (Lk 19:8). He said he would also pay back fourfold anybody whom he had cheated.

A98: (d) Four days (Jn 11:17).

A99: (a, b, c) Praying, fasting and helping the needy (Mt 6:2-6, 16-18).

A100: (a) The rich man who feasted sumptuously every day (Lk 16:19-31).

A101: (b, c, d) Food, drink, and clothing. The Bible says these are things pagans concern themselves with (Mt 6:32). Rather than fretting over tomorrow's needs, we are told by Jesus: "But seek first his kingdom and his righteousness, and all these things shall be yours as well" (Mt 6:33).

Q102: What was the occupation of the man who is usually credited with writing the third and fifth books of the New Testament?
    a. Carpenter
    b. Doctor
    c. Attorney
    d. Tax collector
    e. Governor

Q103: What did St. Stephen, the first Christian martyr, see in the sky just before he was stoned to death?
    a. A dove
    b. A rainbow
    c. Jesus
    d. St. Michael the Archangel
    e. A ring of stars

Q104: After hearing the preaching of the Apostles after Pentecost, what did the owners of fields and houses do?
    a. Invited the poor over
    b. Sold the fields and houses
    c. Used the fields and houses for group prayer
    d. Walked to Jerusalem
    e. Released their slaves

Q105: What happened to the man who sold some property, and kept some money for himself while pretending that he had turned over the entire amount to the Apostles?
    a. He confessed
    b. He collapsed
    c. He clapped
    d. He claimed a profit
    e. He called on the Lord

A102: (b) Doctor. Luke, a physician, has traditionally been credited as the author of the Acts of the Apostles, as well as one of the four Gospel accounts preceding it.

A103: (c) Jesus. Just before his martyrdom, St. Stephen declared: "Behold, I see the heavens opened, and the Son of Man standing at the right hand of God" (Ac 7:56).

A104: (b) They sold their fields and houses and gave the money to the Apostles to be distributed according to needs (Ac 4:34-35).

A105: (b) He collapsed and died. Three hours later, his wife also died, immediately after she lied about whether all the money was turned over to the Apostles (Ac 5:1-11).

Q106: What special day is celebrated 40 days after Easter?
    a. Pentecost
    b. Ascension Thursday
    c. Quinquagesima Sunday
    d. The Assumption
    e. The Annunciation

Q107: What special day arrives 50 days after Easter?
    a. Pentecost
    b. Ascension Thursday
    c. Quinquagesima Sunday
    d. The Assumption
    e. The Annunciation

Q108: Name *three* people in the Bible who fasted for 40 days.
    a. Adam
    b. Moses
    c. Martha
    d. Jesus
    e. Elijah

Q109: Which of the following is not associated with the number 40?
    a. Number of days that St. Francis of Assisi fasted before receiving the stigmata
    b. Number of days that St. Patrick fasted and prayed on the summit of a mountain
    c. Number of days of the Great Flood sent by God during the time of Noah
    d. Number of years the Israelites were condemned to wander around the desert
    e. Number of days baby Isaac was when his father, Abraham, had him circumcised

A106: (b) Ascension Thursday. This is the day Jesus was seen ascending up to heaven from Mount Olivet as disciples watched Jesus rise into the sky until He was hidden by a cloud (Mk 16:19; Lk 24:51). In the United States, many dioceses transfer the celebration of the feast from Thursday to Sunday.

A107: (a) Pentecost. Derived from the Greek word, pentecostes (fiftieth), Pentecost is an ancient Christian feast commemorating the descent of the Holy Spirit upon the Apostles while they were gathered in the Upper Room (Ac 2:1-4). The event occurred on the Jewish Feast of the Pentecost, which was known as the Feast of First Fruits when the Jewish Temple was standing.

A108: (b, d, e) Jesus fasted 40 days in the desert (Mt 4:1-2). In the Old Testament, Moses and Elijah also fasted 40 days (Ex 34:28; 1 K 19:7-8).

A109: (e) In keeping with God's command, Abraham had Isaac circumcised when he was eight days old. Forty is the number associated with Lent, penance, and atonement from sin.

Q110: Why was Moses placed in a basket in the Nile River when he was a baby?
a. To visit his grandmother down the river
b. As a sacrificial offering
c. To protect him
d. To take a bath
e. His parents couldn't feed him

Q111: Which of these Old Testament figures was not an ancestor of Jesus?
a. Adam
b. Abraham
c. Judah
d. David
e. Ishmael

Q112: What is the name of King David's great grandmother?
a. Ruth
b. Aja
c. Abigail
d. Julia
e. Naomi

Q113: The Book of Esther explains the significance and background of which Jewish festival?
a. Shabbatt
b. Sukkot
c. Hanukkah
d. Purim
e. Jerusalem Day

Q114: Who had the longest career as a prophet?
a. Jeremiah
b. Isaiah
c. Amos
d. Ezekiel
e. Hosea

Q115: Everyone has heard of the serpent in the garden of Eden, but which other animal in the Old Testament is represented as speaking?
a. Camel
b. Raven
c. Dove
d. Donkey
e. Lion

A110: (c) The Israelites were slaves in Egypt, and the Pharaoh had ordered the drowning of all male Israelite newborns. The Pharaoh's daughter rescued the child and took him in as her son (Ex 1:22; 2:1-10).

A111: (e) Ishmael was not an ancestor of Jesus, although his half-brother Isaac was. Both were sons of Abraham. The family tree is laid out in the Book of Genesis. It is through Ishmael that Islam declares its people to be descendants of Abraham.

A112: (a) Ruth. Ruth was the mother of Obed, the father of Jesse. Jesse was the father of David. Read about Ruth in the eponymous book of the Old Testament.

A113: (d) Purim is a minor festival that traditionally includes a reading of the Book of Esther. The feast also features noisemakers to drown out the name of Haman (whose plot to annihilate the Jewish people was quashed), costumes, a party, and food for the poor.

A114: (a) Jeremiah. He was a prophet for almost half a century, at least from 627 to 585 A.D. His writings are contained in the Book of Jeremiah in the Old Testament. The three Major Prophets are Isaiah, Jeremiah, and Ezekiel. Minor Prophets include Hosea, Amos, and Micah. They are called "minor" because their writings in the Old Testament are brief.

A115: (d) Donkey. In Numbers 22, we find the account of how the Lord opened the mouth of the donkey who was carrying the pagan seer Balaam, and how she spoke to him.

Q116: Which Old Testament character moved his family from Ur in Babylonia to the city of Haran in Upper Mesopotamia to Canaan to Egypt and back to Canaan?
- a. Adam
- b. Moses
- c. Abraham
- d. Isaac
- e. Cain

Q117: Name the *two* foods that God provided the Israelites while they wandered in the desert.
- a. Figs
- b. Honey
- c. Barley
- d. Manna
- e. Quail

Q118: How old was Abraham when he died?
- a. 50
- b. 75
- c. 100
- d. 175
- e. 225

Q119: When God appeared to Solomon and asked him what he desired from Him, what did Solomon request?
- a. An honest wife
- b. Physical strength
- c. A shining city
- d. Rain to end a drought
- e. Wisdom

Q120: Nearest which sea were the Dead Sea Scrolls discovered in the 20th century?
- a. Red Sea
- b. Black Sea
- c. Sea of Salt
- d. Sea of Galilee
- e. Caspian Sea

Q121: Which are the *two* most mentioned cities in the Bible?
- a. Joppa
- b. Babylon
- c. Jerusalem
- d. Cairo
- e. Carthage

A116: (c) Abraham. Ur is located in present-day Iraq. Canaan encompassed present-day Israel, the West Bank, the Gaza Strip and some other pieces of land.

A117: (d, e) Manna and quail.

A118: (d) 175.

A119: (e) Wisdom in his role as king. God granted the request as He was pleased that Solomon did not ask for things such as possessions, wealth, honor or revenge. See 2 Ch 1:11.

A120: (c) Sea of Salt (or "Dead Sea"). Found in caves along the northwest coast of the sea, the ancient documents include copies of Old Testament books. The Dead Sea Scrolls date back to as early as 250 B.C., though most are dated between 150 B.C. and 70 A.D.

A121: (b, c) Babylon and Jerusalem. The city of Samaria would place third.

Q122: When the Lord called Ezekiel to be a prophet, He told him to eat a particular item before speaking to the people of Israel. What did he have to eat?
    a. A quill pen   d. A holly leaf
    b. A scroll   e. A cicada
    c. Burnt toast

Q123: Along what river in the Middle East did an angel tell Daniel about the future of the kingdoms of Egypt and Syria?
    a. The Euphrates   d. The Indus
    b. The Tigris   e. The Ganges
    c. The Nile

Q124: What kind of wife did the Lord instruct the prophet Hosea to take?
    a. A virgin   d. A pagan
    b. A harlot   e. A child bride
    c. A Jew

Q125: What kind of animal was Jesus riding when he made his triumphal entry into Jerusalem?
    a. Horse   d. Tiger
    b. Elephant   e. Camel
    c. Donkey

Q126: I ate modest meals of locusts and honey. When my mother was pregnant, I leaped inside her womb when a special baby arrived at our house. Who am I?
    a. St. John the Evangelist   d. St. Ann
    b. St. John the Baptist   e. St. Joseph
    c. St. Elizabeth

Q127: Which of these men was not one of the original Twelve Apostles?
    a. St. Bartholomew   d. St. Paul
    b. St. Thaddeus   e. St. Andrew
    c. St. Philip

Q128: How many people saw Jesus after He rose from the dead?
    a. 12   d. 300
    b. 70   e. 500+
    c. 100

Q129: What descended from the sky as Jesus was baptized?
    a. Rain   d. A prophet
    b. The Holy Spirit   e. A meteor
    c. A choir of angels

A122: (b) A scroll. The scroll had writing on both sides and tasted as sweet as honey. (See chapters two and three of Ezekiel).

A123: (b) The Tigris River.

A124: (b) A harlot (Ho 1:2). Later, even while the wife he married was still involved with adultery and prostitution, Hosea was told by the Lord to go back again and love her just as the Lord still loved the people of Israel, despite their turning to other gods (Ho 3:1).

A125: (c) A donkey. Passion (Palm) Sunday commemorates this event, which occurred five days before His crucifixion. The crowds spread tree branches and cloaks along the road. According to the Gospels, they shouted "Hosanna to the Son of David! Blessed is he who comes in the name of the Lord! Hosanna in the highest!" (See Mt 21:1-3, 6-11).

A126: (b) St. John the Baptist. He leaped in the womb of Elizabeth when the Blessed Mother, who was pregnant with the Lord, arrived at the house of his mother and father, Zechariah (Lk 1:41).

A127: (d) St. Paul. Previously known as Saul, St. Paul was called by Jesus after the Resurrection. He was riding his horse on his way to persecute Christians when a blinding light and sound struck him off his horse. The voice of Jesus said to him "Saul, Saul, why do you persecute me?" (Ac 9:4). St. Paul went on to become one of the greatest Apostles.

A128: (e) Jesus was seen by more than 500 people (1 Cor 15:5-6) after He rose from the dead and before He ascended into heaven 40 days later.

A129: (b) The Holy Spirit, in the form of a dove, descended on Jesus from heaven as St. John the Baptist baptized Him.

Q130: When Jesus appeared to the Apostles after the Resurrection, they thought He was a ghost. What did He eat to show them that they were mistaken?

a. Bread

b. Fish

c. Dates

d. Roast lamb

e. Manna

Q131: Who was the last Apostle to die?

a. St. John

b. St. Peter

c. St. Paul

d. St. James

e. St. Andrew

Q132: Jesus changed Simon's name to Peter (or "Cephas" in the original Aramaic). What is the meaning of Cephas?

a. Pebble

b. Rock

c. Wisdom

d. Coward

e. Virtue

Q133: What was the occupation of the Apostle St. Matthew?

a. Tax collector

b. Postal worker

c. Store clerk

d. Farmer

e. Fisherman

Q134: The Apostles were told by Jesus, just before His Ascension into heaven, not to scatter until a significant event occurred. What event?

a. Apocalypse

b. Volcanic eruption

c. Conversion of heathens

d. The arrival of a Counselor sent by the Lord

e. Peace treaty

Q135: What did the Apostles Peter, James and John note about the Lord's appearance at the Transfiguration?

a. He wore a crown

b. He wore a red robe

c. His face shined like the sun

d. He seemed sad

e. He seemed older

A130: (b) We read in Luke 24:41-43 that He ate a piece of cooked fish.

A131: (a) St. John, around the year 100 A.D.

A132: (b) Rock. Jesus, whose everyday language was Aramaic, said to Simon, "So you are Simon the son of John? You shall be called Cephas" (Jn 1:42). In Greek, "petra" means rock, so in that language, Peter was called "Petros" – the masculine form of the feminine noun "petra." Later, Jesus instituted the papacy, saying to Peter, "And I tell you, you are Peter, and on this rock I will build my church, and the powers of death shall not prevail against it. I will give you the keys of the kingdom of heaven, and whatever you bind on earth shall be bound in heaven, and whatever you loose on earth shall be loosed in heaven" (Mt 16:18-19).

A133: (a) Tax collector (Mt 9:9-13).

A134: (d) The arrival of a Counselor sent by the Lord. The Counselor (or "Advocate") was the Holy Spirit, who came ten days after the Ascension on a feast now known as Pentecost. The Holy Spirit descended upon the Apostles in the form of tongues of fire while the Apostles gathered in the Upper Room (Ac 2:1-4).

A135: (c) The Lord's face shined like the sun. At the Transfiguration, three Apostles saw Jesus speaking to Elijah and Moses, who were deceased, on a mountain (Mt 17:1-9).

Chapter Three

History

Q136: Which bridge, connecting Pennsylvania and New Jersey, was named after the Catholic known as the "Father of the American Navy"?
    a. George Washington Bridge
    b. The Commodore Barry Bridge
    c. St. George's Bridge
    d. Benjamin Franklin Bridge
    e. Walt Whitman Bridge

Q137: Which bridge – connecting two boroughs of New York City – was named after a Catholic explorer from Italy?
    a. The Henry Hudson Bridge
    b. The Amerigo Vespucci Bridge
    c. The Joseph Addabbo Memorial Bridge
    d. The Verrazano-Narrows Bridge
    e. The Ponte Vecchio

Q138: What new land did Catholic explorer Jacques Cartier claim for France?
    a. Mexico
    b. Canada
    c. Greenland
    d. Iceland
    e. Alaska

Q139: Which statement about a California city is not correct?
    a. San Francisco was named after St. Francis of Assisi
    b. San Diego was named after St. Diego of Alcala
    c. Santa Barbara was named after St. Barbara
    d. San José was named after St. Joseph
    e. Santa Cruz was named after St. Cruz

Q140: Which Catholic explorer is known as the Founder of Quebec and the Father of New France?
    a. Hernando de Soto
    b. Samuel de Champlain
    c. Francisco Pizarro
    d. Christopher Columbus
    e. Ferdinand Magellan

Q141: Who is known as the discoverer of Lake George?
    a. St. George
    b. King George
    c. St. Isaac Jogues
    d. Balboa
    e. Dora the Explorer

A136: (b) The Commodore Barry Bridge. Spanning the Delaware River, this bridge was named after John Barry (1745-1803), who was a Commodore in the U.S. Navy.

A137: (d) The Verrazano-Narrows Bridge. Connecting Staten Island and Brooklyn at the Narrows, the bridge was named for Giovanni da Verrazano (c. 1485-c. 1528), who is considered the first European navigator to enter the New York Harbor and to explore the mid-Atlantic coast of North America between South Carolina and Newfoundland in 1539, long before the 1609 voyage of Henry Hudson. Verrazano sailed along Long Island Sound and Newport, Rhode Island, both of which are mentioned in a letter by Verrazano that was published in 1556. The letter provides the first description of the North Atlantic coast by a European.

A138: (b) Canada (originally known as New France). Jacques Cartier (1491-1557) was also first to document the name "Canada," derived from the Huron-Iroquois word "kanata," meaning village.

A139: (e) Santa Cruz means "Holy Cross." The list of California cities named after saints is extensive. To give a few examples, Santa Monica was named after St. Monica of Hippo, Santa Clara was named after St. Clare of Assisi, and Santa Ana was named after Jesus' grandmother, St. Anne.

A140: (b) Samuel de Champlain (d. 1635). This French sailor is renowned for his explorations and mapping of Canada and his work to open the way for North American fur trade with France and to fortify Quebec City, where he started a settlement. He discovered Lake Champlain on the border of Vermont and New York State.

A141: (c) St. Isaac Jogues. This Jesuit priest missionary reached the shores of scenic Lake George in 1646 on the eve of the feast of Corpus Christi, prompting the French priest to name the lake "Lac du Saint Sacrament" (Lake of the Blessed Sacrament). The lake, located in the Adirondack Mountains in upstate New York, was later renamed after King George II of Great Britain.

Q142: Who is the patroness of the United States?
- a. St. Elizabeth Ann Seton
- b. St. Frances Xavier Cabrini
- c. St. Kateri Tekakwitha
- d. The Blessed Mother
- e. St. Katharine Drexel

Q143: What event in 1531 converted millions to Christianity in Mexico?
- a. World Fair in Mexico
- b. Papal visit to Mexico
- c. End of famine
- d. Appearance of Virgin Mary
- e. Appearance of angel

Q144: Which Catholic explorer and priest originally named the Mississippi after the Immaculate Conception of Mary?
- a. Juan Ponce de Leon
- b. Jacques Marquette
- c. Cabeza de Vaca
- d. John Cabot
- e. Jacques Cartier

Q145: Which U.S. state was named after a Catholic queen?
- a. Minnesota
- b. Virginia
- c. Maryland
- d. Arizona
- e. Louisiana

Q146: Which U.S. state was named after a Catholic king?
- a. Minnesota
- b. Virginia
- c. Maryland
- d. Arizona
- e. Louisiana

Q147: Which U.S. state has a capital that was named after the Eucharist?
- a. Alaska
- b. Texas
- c. Florida
- d. California
- e. New Mexico

Q148: Name the Washington, D.C.-based organization whose chairman and chief executive is Tim Shriver, a nephew of the late President John F. Kennedy.
- a. Toys for Tots
- b. Special Olympics
- c. Habitat for Humanity
- d. Ronald McDonald House
- e. Make-A-Wish Foundation

Q149: Which U.S. state had its largest city named after the Virgin Mary when the city was founded in 1781?
- a. Alaska
- b. Texas
- c. Florida
- d. California
- e. New Mexico

A142: (d) The Blessed Virgin Mary, under the title "the Immaculate Conception." A major dogma of the Church, the Immaculate Conception refers to the Virgin Mary's conception without sin in the womb of her mother. The young country was consecrated under this title in 1792 by the first Catholic bishop in the United States, John Carroll, who was Bishop of Baltimore. Later, Pope Pius IX made Mary's role more official when he declared the Immaculate Conception to be the Patroness of the United States in 1847.

A143: (d) Appearance of Virgin Mary outside Mexico City to a peasant now known as St. Juan Diego. This apparition of Our Lady of Guadalupe profoundly impacted Mexican culture. A miraculous image of Mary left on St. Juan Diego's tilma (poncho-like piece of clothing) can be viewed at the Basilica of Our Lady of Guadalupe today. Marian apparitions such as this one are not a required belief for the faithful.

A144: (b) Father Jacques Marquette (1636-1675). A Jesuit priest from France, Marquette discovered the upper Mississippi River in 1673 and named it "Conception River."

A145: (c) Maryland. It was named after Henrietta Maria of France (1609-1669), who was princess of France and Queen Consort of England, Scotland and Ireland. She was the French wife of King Charles I and mother of King Charles II and King James II.

A146: (e) Louisiana. It was named after King Louis XIV (1638-1715) by the French Catholic explorer known as La Salle.

A147: (d) California, whose capital is Sacramento, which was named after the Blessed Sacrament. The Spanish explorer, Gabriel Moraga, named the Sacramento River and Sacramento Valley after the same sacrament in the early 1800s.

A148: (b) Special Olympics. Born in 1959, Tim Shriver is the son of the late Sargent Shriver (U.S. vice-presidential candidate in 1972), and Eunice Kennedy Shriver, a younger sister of President Kennedy. Eunice founded the precursor to the Special Olympics in 1962. Tim Shriver, a 1981 Yale University graduate and the father of five, wrote a column entitled "Proud to be Catholic," which appeared April 17, 2008 in *The Washington Post*.

A149: (d) Los Angeles, California's largest city, was originally named El Pueblo de la Reina de Los Ángeles ("The Town of the Queen of Angels") by Felipe de Neve, the Spanish governor of Las Californias.

Q150: Which continent or continents have names based on the baptismal name of a Catholic explorer?
    a. Africa
    b. Asia
    c. Australia
    d. North and South America
    e. Europe

Q151: When Marco Polo arrived near present-day Beijing in 1275, Polo and his father and uncle presented letters to Kublai Khan. From whom were the letters?
    a. King Richard the Lion-hearted
    b. Fra Angelico
    c. St. Thomas Aquinas
    d. Pope Gregory X
    e. St. Bernard

Q152: What was Norse explorer Leif Erickson commissioned to do in Greenland by King Olaf I of Norway?
    a. Claim new lands
    b. Preach Catholicism
    c. Build ships
    d. Print Bibles
    e. Print maps

Q153: What did St. Brendan the Navigator found in Ireland in the sixth century?
    a. A school
    b. Monasteries
    c. A shipyard
    d. The city of Dublin
    e. Maynooth College

Q154: Who or what killed French-born saint St. Isaac Jogues, who helped convert the Indians of Lake Superior?
    a. Sioux Indians
    b. Mohawk Indians
    c. A bear
    d. Smallpox
    e. Freezing temperatures

A150: (d) North and South America were named in honor of Amerigo Vespucci (1454-1512), an Italian navigator.

A151: (d) Pope Gregory X. The Polos also presented Kublai Khan with some oil from the Holy Sepulchre, the tomb in which Christ was laid.

A152: (b) Preach the Catholic faith. Erickson (c. 970-c. 1020) is thought to have landed in North America – specifically, in Newfoundland, Canada – centuries before Christopher Columbus discovered the New World.

A153: (b) Monasteries. Brendan, a monk and saint, was one of the Twelve Apostles of Ireland. He is best known for his semi-legendary journey to the Isle of the Blessed, during which he reportedly encountered a giant sea monster.

A154: (b) Mohawk Indians murdered St. Isaac Jogues (1607-1646). He was canonized a saint on June 29, 1930 along with seven other North American martyrs.

Q155: What did the residents of China realize after Jesuit mathematician Matteo Ricci published world maps with accurate depictions of oceans and landmasses?
  a. That China was not in the Southern Hemisphere
  b. That China was not an island
  c. That China was larger than India
  d. That China was a much smaller part of the world than they had previously thought
  e. That China was adjacent to Russia

Q156: Which body of water was discovered by the Catholic explorer known as Balboa?
  a. The Caribbean Sea
  b. The Pacific Ocean
  c. The Arctic Ocean
  d. Lake Titicaca
  e. New York Harbor

Q157: Who decided to give the name "America" to the New World?
  a. A German cartographer
  b. An Italian navigator
  c. An Asian astronomer
  d. A Spanish linguist
  e. An English buccaneer

Q158: Which Catholic explorer named the Pacific Ocean?
  a. Ferdinand Magellan
  b. Amerigo Vespucci
  c. Christopher Columbus
  d. Hernando de Soto
  e. Pacificus of San Severino

A155: (d) That China was a much smaller part of the world than its citizens had previously thought. It was in 1584 that Ricci, founder of the Catholic missions of China, published these first maps of China and made them available to the western world.

A156: (b) The Pacific Ocean. The Spanish explorer, Vasco Nuñez de Balboa (1475-1517), spotted the Pacific Ocean in 1513 from the western coast of Panama.

A157: (a) A German cartographer and Catholic named Martin Waldseemüller (c. 1470-c. 1521/1522) used the word "America" on his 1507 map, *Universalis Cosmographia*. The name "America" honored the Catholic navigator, Amerigo Vespucci.

A158: (a) Ferdinand Magellan named the ocean (but Balboa discovered it).

Q159: What did the first Church council in Spain forbid new bishops, priests, and deacons from having?
    a. Guns
    b. Gold
    c. Bathing Suits
    d. Wives
    e. Horses

Q160: What became legal in 313 A.D. when the Edict of Milan was issued?
    a. Bibles sales
    b. Liquor sales
    c. Judaism
    d. Christianity
    e. Prayer in schools

Q161: Around 107 A.D., St. Ignatius of Antioch became the first person to use what famous two words together?
    a. Our Father
    b. Hail Mary
    c. Guardian angel
    d. Catholic Church
    e. Ash Wednesday

Q162: How was St. Peter martyred?
    a. Crucifixion
    b. Beheading
    c. Boiling oil
    d. Lions
    e. Bow and arrow

Q163: How was St. Paul martyred?
    a. Crucifixion
    b. Beheading
    c. Boiling oil
    d. Lions
    e. Bow and arrow

A159: (d) Wives. The Council of Elvira, held between 295 A.D. and 302 A.D., required celibacy for all three levels of ordained men. Attended by 18 bishops, the council was the first to be held in Spain.

A160: (d) Christianity. Christianity became a legal religion in the Roman Empire. The edict was issued by Constantine the Great, who was the Emperor.

A161: (d) "Catholic Church." Born in 50 A.D., St. Ignatius was the first of many to refer, in writing, to the entire community of Christians as the Catholic Church.

A162: (a) Legend has it that Peter was crucified upside down.

A163: (b) Paul (as a Roman citizen) was allowed the privilege of being beheaded. This occurred on the road to Ostia, called Via Ostiense.

Q164: Who ordered St. Jerome to translate the Bible into Latin in the late 4th century?
  a. St. Ambrose
  b. Pope Damasus I
  c. Constantine the Great
  d. The Apostles
  e. Martin Luther

Q165: When did the Catholic Church first compile the exact list of New Testament books that are still in the Christian Bible today?
  a. End of 1st century
  b. End of 2nd century
  c. End of 3rd century
  d. End of 4th century
  e. End of 5th century

Q166: Known as the Father of _____, Eusebius was the bishop of Caesarea in Palestine starting around 314 A.D.
  a. Education
  b. Architecture
  c. Church History
  d. Religion
  e. The Bible

Q167: Under my reign as emperor of the Roman Empire, from 284 to 305 A.D., bishops, priests and deacons were jailed and tortured, Christians massacred, and churches destroyed. I appointed Maximian as my Augustus, or co-emperor in 286 A.D. Who am I?
  a. Diocletian
  b. King Herod
  c. Pontius Pilate
  d. Nero
  e. Augustus Caesar

A164: (b) Pope Damasus I.

A165: (d) End of 4th century. The African Councils of Hippo (393 A.D.) and Carthage (397 A.D.) gave us the canon of the Bible, confirming the inspired nature of 27 books that would become our New Testament. For more information on how the Catholic Church determined the contents of the Bible, preserved it through the manual copying by monks, and translated it through the centuries, please read *Where We Got the Bible: Our Debt to the Catholic Church* by Rev. Henry G. Graham.

A166: (c) Church History. Eusebius is the author of *Ecclesiastical History*, which is the most important early historical work on early Christianity.

A167: (a) Diocletian (244-311). His whole name is Gaius Aurelius Valerius Diocletianus. He reigned as Roman Emperor from 284 to 305 A.D. At first, he did little to thwart the growing number of Christians. But later, one of his generals, Galerius, influenced him to become a great persecutor of the Church.

Q168: In the 2ⁿᵈ century, Pope Anicetus decreed that clergy should:
    a. Have short hair
    b. Have long hair
    c. Wear sandals
    d. Go barefoot
    e. Travel on horse

Q169: St. Jerome was commissioned by the pope in the 4th century to translate the Bible into the language of the people. What language was it?
    a. Greek
    b. Latin
    c. Aramaic
    d. Hebrew
    e. English

Q170: Hermeneutics is the art of what?
    a. Being a hermit
    b. Bible interpretation
    c. Organ acoustics
    d. Holy war
    e. Language

Q171: Which of the following is not a famous creed in the Christian tradition?
    a. Nicene Creed
    b. Apostles' Creed
    c. Creed of Pius IV
    d. Athanasian Creed
    e. Geneva Creed

Q172: What powerful king did Pope Leo the Great convince not to conquer Rome?
    a. Attila the Hun
    b. Romulus
    c. Caligula
    d. Nero
    e. Claudius

Q173: Which one of the following groups was *not* a heresy plaguing the Catholic Church during the first five centuries of Christianity?
    a. Nestorianism
    b. Arianism
    c. Pelagianism
    d. Gnosticism
    e. Kabbalah

A168: (a) Clergy should have short hair. St. Anicetus, the eleventh pope, led the Church from 155 to 166 A.D.

A169: (b) Latin.

A170: (b) Hermeneutics is the art or science of Biblical interpretation and explanation.

A171: (e) Geneva Creed. The major Christian creeds included the Nicene Creed (381 A.D.), Apostles' Creed (8th century), Athanasian Creed (4th or 5th century), and the Creed of Pius IV (1564).

A172: (a) Attila, King of the Huns. Pope Leo the Great helped prevent the attack in 452 A.D.

A173: (e) Kabbalah, which is a type of Jewish mysticism. The Kabbalah Centre in Los Angeles, which teaches a modern, New Age interpretation of the ancient method, has attracted Hollywood stars such as Madonna.

Q174: I am the founder of Maryland. I am known as the 2nd Lord Baltimore. The city of Baltimore was named after me. I married Anne Arundell. Who am I?
    a. James Stuart
    b. John Cabot
    c. John Brown
    d. Robert E. Lee
    e. Cecilius Calvert

Q175: My son founded Maryland. My other son was Maryland's first governor. I am known as the 1st Lord Baltimore. I made quite a splash when I converted to Catholicism. Who am I?
    a. George Calvert
    b. Bernie Calvert
    c. James Calvert
    d. Charles Calvert
    e. Paul Calvert

Q176: St. Junípero Serra is known as the "Founder of _____."
    a. California
    b. Oregon
    c. Texas
    d. Hawaii
    e. New Mexico

Q177: John McLoughlin is known as the "Founder of _____."
    a. California
    b. Oregon
    c. Texas
    d. Hawaii
    e. New Mexico

Q178: A U.S. senator for Maryland, Charles Carroll was the only Catholic signer of the _____.
    a. Magna Carta
    b. Mayflower Compact
    c. U.S. Constitution
    d. Declaration of Independence
    e. Treaty of Versailles

A174: (e) Cecilius "Cecil" Calvert (1606-1675). He was the first proprietor of the Maryland colony. Cecil's younger brother, Leonard Calvert (1606-1647), became the first governor of the Province of Maryland, which became the state of Maryland.

A175: (a) George Calvert (1580-1632), 1st Baron Baltimore. This English-born colonizer died five weeks before the sealing of the charter for the settlement of the Maryland colony. His son Cecil inherited the job of settling Maryland. One could say that, in spirit, George Calvert was the true founder of Maryland.

A176: (a) California. Junípero Serra, also known as Padre Serra, was a Franciscan priest whose expeditions in California resulted in the founding of missions that converted multitudes of natives to Christianity. Born on the Spanish island of Majorca in 1713, the missionary, linguist and doctor of theology translated the *Catechism* into the language of the Pame Indians in California. He died in Monterrey, California in 1784.

A177: (b) Oregon. John McLoughlin (1784-1857), a physician and pioneer, joined the Catholic Church in 1842. Born in Canada, McLoughlin was a key figure in the fur trade and the activities of the Hudson's Bay Company.

A178: (d) Declaration of Independence. Charles Carroll (1737-1832) was one of the Founding Fathers of the United States. In 1827, in his old age, he helped create the Baltimore and Ohio Railroad. Monopoly players recognize this rail as the "B & O Railroad."

Q179: Ponce de Leon was a Catholic explorer who is credited with discovering _____ on Easter Sunday in 1513. He was the first governor of Puerto Rico and died in Cuba.
  a. The Fountain of Youth
  b. Florida
  c. Georgia
  d. Alabama
  e. The Dominican Republic

Q180: Ferdinand Magellan was a Catholic explorer who was credited with being the first to:
  a. Swim from Cuba to Florida
  b. Sail from Mexico to Florida
  c. Circumnavigate the globe
  d. See the North Pole
  e. See the Rocky Mountains

Q181: What historic gift was received by William R. Grace in 1885 while he was mayor of New York City?
  a. Central Park
  b. The Brooklyn Bridge
  c. Coney Island Ferris Wheel
  d. Statue of Liberty
  e. Atlas Statue

Q182: What was the first Christian worship service held in the continental United States?
  a. A Methodist revival
  b. A Baptist service
  c. A Catholic Mass
  d. An Anglican liturgy
  e. A Puritan prayer meeting

Q183: In what American city was the standard text used in U.S. Catholic school religion classes from the 1880s to the late 1960s produced in?
  a. Chicago
  b. Boston
  c. Philadelphia
  d. New York
  e. Baltimore

A179: (b) Florida. The Spanish explorer Ponce de Leon (1460-1521) named the peninsula "Florida," meaning "flowery." He never did find the rumored Fountain of Youth for which he searched. Although Ponce de Leon is officially credited with finding Florida, records indicate that other Europeans probably reached it earlier.

A180: (c) Circumnavigate the globe. Portuguese by birth, Magellan (1480-1521) sailed around the world for Spain. The waterway he found that cut across the southern tip of South America is known as the Strait of Magellan. The odd birds spotted by the explorer and his crew are known as Magellanic penguins. Although it sounds paradoxical, Magellan was killed during his expedition around the world but he was still the first man to go completely around the earth. On an earlier voyage sailing east, he reached the island of Banda. On the westward voyage around the world, he was killed on the island of Cebu, 5° west of Banda. The surviving members of his crew were the first men ever to go around the world on one continuous voyage.

A181: (d) The Statue of Liberty (from France). Grace, the first Catholic mayor of New York City, went to Mass every morning before work, according to the original *Catholic Encyclopedia* (1909).*

A182: (c) Catholic Mass. Hundreds of Catholic Masses would have been celebrated throughout Florida in the early 1500s, such as by the missionary priests who accompanied Ponce de Leon to Florida. But the first documented Mass at a permanent mission – Mission Nombre de Dios – was celebrated in 1565 by Fr. Martin Francisco Lopez de Mendoza Grajales in St. Augustine, Florida.

A183: (e) Baltimore. The most common edition of the *Baltimore Catechism* is in question-answer format and comes replete with Bible quotes.

* www.newadvent.org/cathen/06714a.htm

Q184: My inventing the printing press in my home country of Germany means we can print Bibles instead of waiting for monks to copy them by hand. Who am I?

    a. Johann Gutenberg

    b. Gottfried Leibniz

    c. Carl Benz

    d. Prince Hermann

    e. Immanuel Kant

Q185: My coins have the letter "C" or "M." My mother was St. Helena. From a vision, I saw clearly I should be Christian and conquer in the name of Christ. Who am I?

    a. Constantine the Great

    b. St. Francis of Assisi

    c. St. Patrick

    d. Maxentius

    e. Flavian

Q186: I established the Secretariate of Indian Affairs to protect Native Americans from overzealous colonists in the New World. Who am I?

    a. George Washington

    b. Alexander Hamilton

    c. Ben Franklin

    d. Queen Isabella of Spain

    e. Richard III

Q187: Which Doctor of the Church is known as "the Father of English history"?

    a. The Venerable Bede

    b. John Henry Newman

    c. Sir Walter Raleigh

    d. Charles Cornwallis

    e. Oliver Cromwell

Q188: Name the excommunicated Catholic who wrote a letter on Feb. 9, 1812, in which he stated his refusal to free Pope Pius VII, who was being held captive in France.

    a. Mussolini

    b. Napoleon

    c. Machiavelli

    d. Stalin

    e. Lenin

Q189: Who was the famous cardinal who became Secretary of State in his country in 1616 and was a main character in the 1844 novel, *The Three Musketeers*?

    a. McGwire

    b. Sheen

    c. Richelieu

    d. Wolsey

    e. Mazarin

A184: (a) Johann Gutenberg (born c. 1400, died 1467 or 1468). Born in Mainz, Germany, this Catholic inventor used his new printing press invention to create the beautiful Gutenberg Bible. It is believed that at the end of his life, he was a tertiary, i.e., a follower of the Rule of the Third Order of St. Francis.

A185: (a) Constantine the Great. During the Great Persecution, Constantine (306-337), the Roman Emperor had a vision of a cross in the sky on the eve of battle against Emperor Maxentius. The cross bore the inscription "IN HOC VINCES" ("in this sign wilt thou conquer"). Constantine placed the cross on the shields of his soldiers, and won the battle. The practice of Christianity would henceforth be tolerated in the empire.

A186: (d) Queen Isabella of Spain. Married to King Ferdinand, Isabella the Catholic saw to it that Christopher Columbus received the funding and ships he needed for his famous 1492 expedition to the New World, and later took steps to protect the American Indians.

A187: (a) The Venerable Bede (died 735). This priest and monk authored the *Ecclesiastical History of the English People*, providing an account of Christianity in England from the beginning up to his own time. The work cites many miracles in England that helped convert the people to the Catholic faith.

A188: (b) Napoleon I (Bonaparte).

A189: (c) Cardinal Richelieu (1585-1642). After being named Secretary of State in France in 1616, the French bishop became a cardinal in 1622 and King Louis XIII's chief minister in 1624, a position that helped him shape the future of France. In 1638, he prompted the king to consecrate France to the Virgin Mary. The cardinal is buried in Paris under the Chapel of the Sorbonne, the historic college founded in 1253 with the pope's approval and which the cardinal rebuilt in the 1600s.

Chapter Four
Saints

Q190: In which United States East Coast city are the remains of Mother Cabrini displayed behind glass?
  a. New York City   d. Chicago
  b. Philadelphia   e. Hartford
  c. Baltimore

Q191: Of which United States East Coast diocese was St. John Neumann bishop from 1852 to 1860?
  a. New York City   d. Chicago
  b. Philadelphia   e. Hartford
  c. Baltimore

Q192: In which United States East Coast city did St. Katharine Drexel grow up?
  a. New York City   d. Chicago
  b. Philadelphia   e. Hartford
  c. Baltimore

Q193: In which American city on the East Coast was St. Elizabeth Seton born?
  a. New York City   d. Chicago
  b. Philadelphia   e. Hartford
  c. Baltimore

Q194: In which United States Midwestern state did St. Theódore Guérin found the liberal arts college, Saint Mary-of-the-Woods College?
  a. Wisconsin   d. Iowa
  b. Indiana   e. Kansas
  c. Ohio

Q195: On October 9, 2009, President Barack Obama announced he was sending a six-member delegation to the Vatican for the canonization of which Catholic saint?
  a. Damien de Veuster
  b. Kateri Tekakwitha
  c. Marianne Cope
  d. Theodore Guérin
  e. Dorothy Day

A190: (a) New York City. Known as Mother Cabrini, the Italian-born St. Frances Xavier Cabrini was the first American citizen to be canonized a saint.

A191: (b) Philadelphia. St. John Neumann was the first American bishop to be canonized. Today, his body is displayed behind glass at St. Peter the Apostle Church in Philadelphia.

A192: (b) Philadelphia. St. Katharine Drexel (1858-1955) devoted herself to the poor and oppressed, especially Native Americans and blacks in the South and Southwest. She became the second American-born saint to be canonized.

A193: (a) New York City. Considered a patron saint of Catholic schools, St. Elizabeth Ann Seton (1774-1821) founded the American Sisters of Charity in Emmetsburg, Maryland, where the saint's shrine is located today. She was the first American-born saint to be canonized.

A194: (b) Indiana. The French-born St. Theódore Guérin (1798-1856) was canonized by Pope Benedict XVI in 2006.

A195: (a) Fr. Damien de Veuster (1840-1889), a Belgian priest who devoted his life to working with patients afflicted with leprosy (also called Hansen's disease) in Hawaii. Having lived in Hawaii as a child, President Obama said he could recall many stories from his youth about the saint's tireless work with lepers. Fr. Damien was canonized on October 11, 2009.

Q196: What does the Blessed Mother have in heaven that the rest of us will not have in heaven until the Last Day?
a. A white robe
b. A legion of angels
c. Her soul
d. Her body
e. Wings

Q197: Who designed the Miraculous Medal, which has been worn around the necks of millions of Catholics?
a. St. Simon Stock
b. St. Catherine Labouré
c. Betsy Ross
d. The Virgin Mary
e. Gloria Vanderbilt

Q198: When the pregnant Blessed Mother showed up at Elizabeth's house, Elizabeth's baby leaped inside her womb. Who was the baby?
a. St. Peter
b. St Matthew
c. St. John the Baptist
d. St. Martha
e. Lazarus

Q199: Who told the Blessed Mother to name her Son Jesus?
a. Mary's mother
b. Mary's husband, St. Joseph
c. Mary's cousin, St. Elizabeth
d. The Angel Gabriel
e. The Angel Michael

A196: (d) Her body. This major Church dogma is called the Assumption of Mary. Unlike Mary, other souls in heaven will have to wait until the Last Day (Judgment Day) for the reunification of their souls and bodies, which separate at the point of death. At the end of Mary's life, God took both her body and soul into heaven (*Catechism of the Catholic Church* #966).

A197: (d) The Virgin Mary. The Miraculous Medal (or "Medal of the Immaculate Conception"), was designed by the Blessed Mother, who appeared to St. Catherine Labouré in 1830 and told her to have a medal struck with the image she showed her. Mary said those who wore it around their necks would receive great graces. Please note that apparitions of the Virgin Mary over the centuries are not part of the deposit of faith, which ended with the death of the last Apostle, and in no way should be considered dogma or required belief for the faithful. Private revelations – even those recognized by the Church – do not belong to the deposit of faith. "It is not their role to improve or complete Christ's definitive Revelation, but to help live more fully by it in a certain period of history" (*Catechism of the Catholic Church* #67).

A198: (c) St. John the Baptist, who was Jesus' cousin.

A199: (d) The Angel Gabriel (Lk 1:26-38).

Q200: What Biblical event is considered the first intercession of the Blessed Mother?
  a. Miracle at Cana
  b. Raising of Lazarus
  c. Feeding of the Five Thousand
  d. Last Supper
  e. Walking on Water

Q201: What did the Blessed Mother instruct St. Dominic to do when she appeared to him?
  a. Make a pilgrimage
  b. Translate the Bible
  c. Spread rosary devotion
  d. Build a school
  e. Become a bishop

Q202: Which one of these sites of claimed apparitions of Mary was never approved by the Catholic Church?
  a. Međugorje
  b. Lourdes
  c. Guadalupe
  d. Fatima
  e. Knock

Q203: What special thing remains to this day at the site where the Blessed Mother appeared to St. Bernadette in France in the 1850s?
  a. Photo of the Blessed Mother
  b. Healing waters
  c. A cherry tree
  d. A shadow
  e. Ancient map

A200: (a) The miraculous changing of water into wine at the Wedding of Cana (Jn 2:1-11). After Jesus was approached by His mother about the wine having run out, He worked His first recorded miracle.

A201: (c) To preach the rosary to fight heresy and sin. St. Dominic, who died in 1221, is the founder of the Order of Preachers (OP), whose members are known as the Dominicans.

A202: (a) Međugorje. Unlike Lourdes (France), Guadalupe (Mexico), Fatima (Portugal), and Knock (Ireland), Međugorje (present-day Bosnia and Herce-govina) is not the site of any Church-approved apparitions, despite claims of them continuing since 1981. The bishop whose jurisdiction includes Međugorje has asked the alleged visionaries to stop claiming they have been seeing the Virgin Mary.

A203: (b) A healing spring. The miraculous spring still exists in Lourdes, France, where the Blessed Mother appeared to St. Bernadette. Thousands of miraculous cures have been reported there, including 68 declared by the Church to be medically inexplicable.

Q204: St. Augustine wrote: "I would not believe in the Gospel if the authority of the _____ did not move me to do so."
    a. Bible
    b. Catechism
    c. Catholic Church
    d. Christian Church
    e. Word of God

Q205: St. Augustine wrote: "A man cannot have salvation except in the _____."
    a. Catholic Church
    b. Christian Church
    c. Word of God
    d. Grace of God
    e. Absence of sin

Q206: What does St. Augustine refer to as "the heaviest offense of all"?
    a. Striking one's brother
    b. Blasphemy
    c. Schism
    d. Stealing
    e. Immodesty

Q207: According to St. Augustine, "Who is ignorant that the first of the Apostles is the most blessed _____?"
    a. Peter
    b. Paul
    c. James
    d. John
    e. Andrew

Q208: According to St. Augustine, "God does not forgive sins except to the _____."
    a. Baptized
    b. Confirmed
    c. Married
    d. True believers
    e. Pious

Q209: In view of the fact that sins require atonement, what does St. Augustine suggest we do after sinning?
    a. Apologize
    b. Read the Bible
    c. Read the Catechism
    d. Say a Hail Mary
    e. Punish ourselves before God punishes us

Q210: According to St. Augustine, one cannot enter heaven without which *two* sacraments?
    a. Baptism
    b. Anointing of the Sick
    c. Holy Orders
    d. Confirmation
    e. Eucharist

A204: (c) Catholic Church. Source: *Against the Letter of Mani called "The Foundation"* 5:6 (397 A.D.).

A205: (a) Catholic Church. Source: *Discourse to the People of Caesarea*, 6 (418 A.D.). The reader should keep in mind that the Catholic Church has not accepted all of St. Augustine's theological opinions without further clarifications. On this point see the *Catechism of the Catholic Church* ##846-848, 1257-1261.

A206: (c) Schism. (See St. Augustine's work, *On Baptism, Against the Donatists* (2:7).

A207: (a) Peter.

A208: (a) Baptized. Source: *Sermon to Catechumens, On the Creed* 7:15 (395 A.D.). Again, see the *Catechism* citation in A205.

A209: (e) Punish ourselves before God punishes us. "Sin cannot go unpunished. It would be unseemly, improper, and unjust for sin to go unpunished. Since, therefore, sin must not go unpunished, let it be punished by you, lest you be punished for it… do not put it behind you, or God will put it in front of you" (*Sermons* 20:2 [410 A.D.]).

A210: (a, e) Baptism and the Eucharist. "The Churches of Christ hold inherently that without baptism and participation at the table of the Lord it is impossible for any man to attain either to the kingdom of God or to salvation and life eternal. This is the witness of Scripture too" (*Forgiveness and the Just Deserts of Sin, and the Baptism of Infants* 1:24:34 [412 A.D.]). Yet again, see the *Catechism* citation in A205. "God has bound salvation to the sacrament of Baptism, but he himself is not bound by his sacraments" (*Catechism* #1257).

Q211: St. Ambrose of Milan wrote: "Where _____ is, there is the Church."
    a. Prayer
    b. Peter
    c. Paul
    d. The preacher
    e. The assembly

Q212: St. Cyprian of Carthage wrote: "If he [should] desert the _____ upon whom the Church was built, can he still be confident that he is in the Church?"
    a. Bible
    b. Council of Elders
    c. Reformation
    d. Chair of Peter
    e. Church Fathers

Q213: According to St. Ignatius of Antioch, those who oppose the mind of God "do not confess that the Eucharist is the _____ of our Savior Jesus Christ."
    a. Flesh
    b. Symbol
    c. Celebration
    d. Reminder
    e. Teaching

A211: (b) Peter. The quote is from St. Ambrose's *Commentary on Twelve Psalms of David* written in 389 A.D.

A212: (d) Chair of Peter. This is the office held by the pope or direct successor of St. Peter. The quote is from St. Cyprian's *The Unity of the Catholic Church* (251 A.D.).

A213: (a) Flesh. "Take note of those who hold heterodox opinions on the grace of Jesus Christ which has come to us, and see how contrary their opinions are to the mind of God.... They abstain from the Eucharist and from prayer because they do not confess that the Eucharist is the flesh of our Savior Jesus Christ, flesh which suffered for our sins and which that Father, in His goodness, raised up again. They who deny the gift of God are perishing in their disputes" (*Letter to the Smyrnaeans* 6:2-7:1 [110 A.D.]).

Q214: St. John Chrysostom wrote: "_____ have received a power which God has given neither to angels nor to archangels."
    a. Teachers
    b. Husbands
    c. Priests
    d. Judges
    e. Prophets

Q215: According to St. Irenaeus, what should we point out to prove that our Church has the tradition and faith of the Apostles?
    a. Origin of the Bible
    b. Apostolic succession
    c. Certain prayers
    d. Justification by Faith
    e. Church architecture

Q216: According to St. Justin Martyr, what is "both the flesh and blood of that incarnated Jesus"?
    a. The Eucharist
    b. Prayer
    c. Scripture
    d. Confirmation
    e. Marriage

A214: (c) Priests (*The Priesthood* 3:5:182-183 [c. 387 A.D.]).

A215: (b) Apostolic succession (the successions of our current bishops from the Apostles). "We shall confound all those who... assemble other than where it is proper, by pointing out here the successions of the bishops of the greatest and most ancient Church known to all, founded and organized at Rome by the two most glorious apostles, Peter and Paul – that Church which has the tradition and the faith with which comes down to us after having been announced to men by the apostles. For with this Church, because of its superior origin, all churches must agree, that is, all the faithful in the whole world. And it is in her that the faithful everywhere have maintained the apostolic tradition" (*Against Heresies* 3:3:2 [189 A.D.]).

A216: (a) The Eucharist. Justin Martyr wrote that "the food which has been made into the Eucharist by the Eucharistic prayer set down by him, and by the change of which our blood and flesh is nurtured, is both the flesh and the blood of that incarnated Jesus" (*First Apology* 66 [151 A.D.]).

Q217: What great event in St. Padre Pio's life occurred after the saint offered himself as a sacrifice for an end to World War I?
- a. He levitated
- b. He cured the sick
- c. He became bishop
- d. He won the Nobel Prize
- e. He received the stigmata

Q218: Why did the Italian monk and stigmatist St. Padre Pio (1887-1968) appear in the sky during WWII?
- a. To stop a dangerous storm
- b. To ease people's worries
- c. To be closer to God
- d. To protect people from bombs
- e. He loved birds

Q219: Why was St. Joseph of Cupertino (1603-1663) known as the "Flying Friar"?
- a. He previously was a bomber pilot
- b. He was an Olympian high jumper
- c. He levitated frequently
- d. He wore a cape
- e. He climbed trees

Q220: What do St. Teresa of Avila (1515-1582), St. Thérèse of Lisieux (1873-1897), and St. Catherine of Siena (1347-1380) have in common?
- a. They all are Doctors of the Church
- b. They all hailed from Belgium
- c. They all founded convents
- d. They all lived to be 90
- e. They all died by age 25

Q221: What did St. Francis of Assisi see coming from the sky just before he received his stigmata?
- a. A flaming winged figure
- b. Meteors
- c. One hundred doves
- d. A tornado
- e. Tongues of fire

Q222: What good news did an angel bring to St. Patrick on a mountain?
- a. He would go to heaven soon
- b. He would be canonized a saint
- c. The war would end soon
- d. The Second Coming would occur in Ireland
- e. Multitudes of people in Ireland would be saved

Q223: What is so special about St. Faustina's diary?
- a. It does not fade with time
- b. It contains everything the Lord told the saint
- c. An angel transcribed it
- d. It was written in a previously unknown language
- e. It predicts the date of the Apocalypse

A217: (e) He received the stigmata from Christ. The stigmata are the wounds left in Christ's body from the crucifixion.

A218: (d) To prevent Allied bombers from bombing his hometown in Italy, Padre Pio, who died in 1968, appeared in the sky above his hometown of San Giovanni Rotondo to prevent the American bombers from dropping bombs. It worked. The pilots returned to base explaining to their commander that a giant monk in the sky was stopping them.

A219: (c) Because he levitated frequently. The saint's levitations were witnessed by hundreds, including Pope Urban VIII and two cardinals. He once levitated to the top of St. Peter's Basilica for two hours.

A220: (a) All three women were declared Doctors of the Church.

A221: (a) St. Francis saw a figure with flaming wings coming down from the sky, appearing crucified with bleeding wounds. The figure had the face of Jesus and Jesus spoke to the saint. The incident occurred on Mount Alverna shortly after St. Francis asked the Lord to experience His suffering and love inside him. Brother Leo, one of the saint's three companions on the mountain, left a written account of the event.

A222: (e) The angel announced that salvation had been won for multitudes in Ireland thanks to the harsh penances and prayer of St. Patrick (387-c. 460 A.D.).

A223: (b) The famous diary contains everything the Lord Jesus told this saint, in His own words. St. Faustina Kowalska (1905-1938) was the Polish nun through whom Jesus communicated His message of Divine Mercy.

Q224: According to St. John Chrysostom, what special thing did God give to priests that not even angels had?
    a. Ability to read souls
    b. Ability to see the future
    c. The power to forgive sins
    d. White robes
    e. Assurance of salvation

Q225: Who became known as the "Wonder-worker of England" for the quantity and magnitude of his miracles in the seventh century?
    a. St. Thomas More
    b. St. Thomas Becket
    c. St. Cuthbert
    d. St. Anselm of Canterbury
    e. St. Boniface

Q226: St. Bridget of Sweden, the renowned mystic of the 14th century, had visions of the _____ that strongly influenced religious paintings of the 14th and 15th centuries.
    a. Nativity
    b. Miracle at Cana
    c. Resurrection
    d. Last Supper
    e. Apocalypse

Q227: Who was the first saint from the New World to be canonized?
    a. St. Rose of Lima
    b. St. John Neumann
    c. St. Frances Xavier Cabrini
    d. St. Elizabeth Ann Seton
    e. St. Juan Diego

Q228: St. Gianna Molla was the first woman _____ to be canonized a saint by the Catholic Church.
    a. Lawyer   d. Astronomer
    b. Physician   e. Sculptor
    c. Engineer

Q229: Which of the following saints was not a mother?
    a. St. Elizabeth of Hungary   d. St. Rosalia
    b. St. Monica   e. St. Anne
    c. St. Helena

A224: (c) The power to forgive sins. Jesus said to His Apostles: "Whose sins you forgive are forgiven them, and whose sins you retain are retained" (Jn 20:23). Referring to this power, St. John Chrysostom wrote: "Priests have received a power which God has given neither to angels nor to archangels..." (*The Priesthood* 3:5 [387 A.D.]).

A225: (c) St. Cuthbert. The body of St. Cuthbert, a bishop, monk, and evangelizer of north England, remained incorrupt for many centuries.

A226: (a) Nativity. On God's command, St. Bridget of Sweden founded the Brigittine Order of nuns to reform the monastic life in her country. She is the mother of St. Catherine of Sweden.

A227: (a) St. Rose of Lima (1586-1617). According to the saint's writings, Jesus told her, "Let all men know that grace comes after tribulation. Let them know that without the burden of afflictions it is impossible to reach the height of grace."

A228: (b) Physician. When St. Gianna Beretta Molla (1922-1962) was pregnant and was suffering from a serious medical condition, doctors recommended abortion, but the saint refused, offering this famous response: "If you must decide between me and the child, do not hesitate: choose the child – I insist on it. Save him." The Italian saint died a week after giving birth to a baby girl, Gianna Emanuela, who, like her mother, became a physician.

A229: (d) St. Rosalia, a probable descendant of Charlemagne, was not a mother. Out of love for God, she left home to live in a cave. St. Anne was the mother of the Virgin Mary. St. Helena was the mother of Constantine. St. Monica was the mother of St. Augustine. St. Brigid, St. Felicity, and St. Elizabeth of Hungary were also mothers.

Chapter Five

Papacy

Q230: How many men have "sat" in the Chair of Peter, that is to say, served as pope?

    a. 65   d. 365

    b. 165   e. 1,065

    c. 266

Q231: Who was the second pope?

    a. Leo   d. Lawrence

    b. Louis   e. Leopold

    c. Linus

Q232: What was the home country of Pope John Paul II?

    a. Germany   d. Finland

    b. Poland   e. England

    c. Italy

Q233: What was the home country of Pope Benedict XVI?

    a. Germany

    b. Poland

    c. Italy

    d. Finland

    e. England

Q234: Which of the following is *not* true about Pope Francis?

    a. He used to dance the tango with his former girlfriend

    b. He is a Franciscan

    c. Spanish and Italian are the languages he speaks most fluently

    d. He is a fan of soccer and author Jorge Luis Borges

    e. He became the first pope from the Americas

Q235: Pope Adrian IV was the only pope from which European country?

    a. Egypt

    b. England

    c. Netherlands

    d. Denmark

    e. Finland

A230: (c) 266. According to the *Annuario Pontificio*, the Vatican's yearly directory, Pope Francis would be the 266th pope. If one counted Stephen II, who was elected pope in 752 A.D., but who died before he was consecrated, then Pope Francis would be 267th.

A231: (c) St. Linus was the first to succeed St. Peter as pope (bishop of Rome) in the first century. The third and fourth bishops of Rome were St. Cletus and St. Clement of Rome.

A232: (b) Poland. Pope John Paul II was the first non-Italian pope in 455 years. The native lands of previous popes have included Spain, Portugal, France, Palestine, Syria, Greece, Africa, and most of all, Italy.

A233: (a) Germany.

A234: (b) Pope Francis is not a Franciscan, but a Jesuit (member of the Society of Jesus, which is a religious order of priests and brothers). He became Archbishop of Buenos Aires, Argentina in 1998 and a cardinal in 2001. He was elected pope on March 13, 2013 at the age of 76. He chose his papal name for St. Francis of Assisi.

A235: (b) England. Pope from 1154 to 1159, Adrian IV handed Ireland over to King Henry II of England.

Q236: Which are the titles of two plays written by Pope John Paul II and which were later filmed?
- a. *Our God's Brother*
- b. *The Jeweler's Shop*
- c. *The Artist's Canvas*
- d. *Bella*
- e. *Padre on Horseback*

Q237: What was Pope John Paul II's name before he was pope?
- a. Albino Luciani
- b. Pierre Roger
- c. Adrian Boeyens
- d. Karol Wojtyla
- e. Joseph Ratzinger

Q238: What was Pope Benedict XVI's name before he was pope?
- a. Albino Luciani
- b. Pierre Roger
- c. Adrian Boeyens
- d. Karol Wojtyla
- e. Joseph Ratzinger

Q239: How long did Pope John Paul II serve as pope?
- a. 5½ years
- b. 10½ years
- c. 15½ years
- d. 21½ years
- e. 26½ years

A236: (a, b) *Our God's Brother* and *The Jeweler's Shop.*

A237: (d) Karol Wojtyla.

A238: (e) Joseph Ratzinger.

A239: (e) 26½ years (October 1978-April 2005). It was not the longest papacy. The two longest were those of St. Peter the Apostle (about 35 years, from 32 to 67 A.D.) and Pope Pius IX (about 31½ years, from 1846 to 1878). Next in line would be Pope Leo XIII (25 years), Pope Pius VI (24½ years), Pope Adrian I (almost 24 years), and Pope Pius XII (23½ years).

Q240: Which is not true about Gregorian Chant?
   a. It was named after Pope Gregory the Great, pope from 590 to 604
   b. It influenced the development of medieval and Renaissance music
   c. The chants were sung by monks in monasteries but never by the faithful at Mass
   d. The music is vocal and monophonic (having melody yet no harmony)
   e. Charlemagne spread the chants through his Roman Empire

Q241: Who was the first monk to become pope?
   a. St. Gregory the Great
   b. St. Pius X
   c. St. Benedict of Nursia
   d. St. Innocent XIII
   e. St. John Paul I

Q242: In a decree issued 607 A.D., what did Pope Boniface III prohibit during the first three days after the death of a pope?
   a. The funeral
   b. Dancing
   c. Crying
   d. Eating
   e. Preparations for appointing the next pope

Q243: Which of the following is *not* a theme in Pope Leo the Great's writings in the 5th century?
   a. The evils of Pelagianism
   b. The primacy of the Bishop of Rome
   c. Church unity
   d. Inability to lose salvation
   e. Rising above earthly things

Q244: In which century was Roger Bacon commissioned to write the *Opus Majus*, an 840-page treatise on natural science, mathematics, physics, philosophy, logic, languages, alchemy, the manufacture of gun powder, the positions of celestial bodies, and future inventions such as telescopes and flying machines?
   a. 2nd century
   b. 5th century
   c. 7th century
   d. 10th century
   e. 13th century

A240: (c) is incorrect because Gregorian Chant *was* sung at Masses, and continues to be. Gregorian Chant is deemed the most sacred music of the Church.

A241: (a) Pope Gregory the Great, who died in 604 A.D.

A242: (e) Discussions or plans for the appointment of a successor to the deceased pope. The punishment for a violation was excommunication.

A243: (d) The inability to lose one's salvation was not, and is not, a theme of any papal or Church document, and is counter to the teaching of the Church. The text of 96 sermons and 143 letters written by Pope Leo the Great in the 5th century have survived to the present day and can be read by all!

A244: (e) 13th century. One of the greatest 13th century thinkers, Roger Bacon was one of the earliest European advocates of the scientific method. Surnamed "Doctor Mirabilis" (Wonderful Teacher), Bacon was an English philosopher and scientist and was one of the most well-known Franciscan friars of his time. Bacon was commissioned by Pope Clement IV to write the masterpiece.

Q245: In 609 A.D. what did Pope Boniface IV turn the Pantheon into?
- a. A convent
- b. A museum
- c. The governor's office
- d. A Christian church
- e. A lion's den

Q246: In which German city did Pope Benedict XVI once serve as archbishop?
- a. Berlin
- b. Munich
- c. Bonn
- d. Frankfurt
- e. Hamburg

Q247: What feast does the Church celebrate on February 22?
- a. Feast of the Chair of Peter
- b. Feast of the Bed of Bartholomew
- c. Feast of the Pot of Paul
- d. Feast of the Table of James
- e. Feast of the Altar of Andrew

Q248: What unpleasant experience did more than half of the popes between 33 A.D. and 258 A.D. share?
- a. Persecution
- b. Martyrdom
- c. Daily rainfall
- d. Holy wars
- e. Bankruptcy

A245: (d) He turned it into a Christian church (from a pagan temple), and then consecrated it to the Virgin Mary and all the martyrs. Built in 27 B.C., the Pantheon had been dedicated to Roman gods such as Jupiter, Venus and Mars. Today, the Pantheon serves as a Catholic church.

A246: (b) Munich, the capital of Bavaria, Germany. Later, from 1981 to 2005, Cardinal Ratzinger was head of the Congregation for the Doctrine of the Faith. He was elected pope in 2005.

A247: (a) Feast of the Chair of Peter. This feast, celebrated even in the first few centuries of Christianity, celebrates the special office of authority that has been passed down from Peter through the popes. In the early days, the feast featured veneration of an actual chair in which the Apostle St. Peter had sat in "as presiding officer of the assembly of the faithful," according to the original *Catholic Encyclopedia* (1908).*

A248: (b) Martyrdom.

* www.newadvent.org/cathen/03551e.htm

Q249: How old was Pope Benedict XVI when he was elected pope in 2005?
  a. 68
  b. 72
  c. 78
  d. 82
  e. 88

Q250: Whose doctrine was the focus of Pope Benedict XVI's doctoral thesis?
  a. St. Augustine
  b. St. Thomas Aquinas
  c. Aristotle
  d. Plato
  e. Pope John Paul II

Q251: What was the occupation of Pope Benedict XVI's father?
  a. Farmer
  b. Tour guide
  c. Police officer
  d. Musician
  e. Costume designer

Q252: What does Pope Benedict XVI's older brother Georg do?
  a. He is a tour guide
  b. He is a priest
  c. He is a butler
  d. He is a cook
  e. He drives a bus

A249: (c) He was 78. He became the oldest elected pope since Pope Clement XII in 1730.

A250: (a) St. Augustine. The title of the Pope Benedict's thesis was "The People and House of God in St. Augustine's doctrine of the Church."

A251: (c) Police officer. The pope's father came from a family of farmers in Lower Bavaria and was also a musician who conducted the cathedral choir of Regensburg, Germany.

A252: (b) He is a priest. Born in 1924, Msgr. Georg Ratzinger attended seminary with the future pope. Pope Benedict also had an older sister, Maria Ratzinger, who never married. She died in 1991.

Q253: Vatican City is the smallest country in the world. Which of the following is closest to it in size?
a. Rhode Island
b. Atlantic City
c. The Mall in Washington, D.C.
d. Kuwait
e. Luxembourg

Q254: Which of the following is not true about Peter's Pence?
a. It is a significant source of financial support for Vatican City
b. This annual collection is taken up at Catholic churches all over the world
c. It is a voluntary donation that goes straight to Rome instead of a local parish
d. It is collected on or near the Solemnity of Sts. Peter and Paul (June 29)
e. Italy is usually the largest contributor

Q255: What type of government would you find in Vatican City?
a. Democracy
b. Oligarchy
c. Robocracy
d. Absolute monarchy
e. Anarchy

Q256: Which treaty gave Vatican City independence from Italy in 1929?
a. Lateran
b. Luna
c. Melfi
d. Constance
e. Versailles

Q257: *Codex Vaticanus* and *Codex Sinaiticus* are the world's oldest _____.
a. Concordats
b. Bibles
c. Monasteries
d. Greek dictionaries
e. Latin textbooks

A253: (c) The Mall.

A254: (e) The United States – not Italy – usually provides the greatest percentage of the donation each year.

A255: (d) Absolute monarchy. The pope, who serves as Bishop of Rome, is the absolute monarch. If he has been secretly replaced by an android, then it would be a robocracy. (One of my editors made me put this in. He just likes using robocracy in an answer.)

A256: (a) The Lateran Treaty consisted of three main parts: a treaty recognizing the Holy See's sovereignty in the newly established Vatican City state; a concordat regulating the Catholic Church's position in Italy; and a financial convention settling the claims of the Holy See after its loss of land.

A257: (b) Bibles. Both were handwritten in Greek in the 4th century. The *Codex Vaticanus* is preserved at the Vatican Library, which contains about 75,000 manuscripts and more than a million printed books. The *Codex Sinaiticus* can be examined at www.codexsinaiticus.org. It was discovered by Constantine Tischendorf at the Monastery of St. Catherine at Mount Sinai.

Chapter Six
Science

Q258: What famous theory about the world was proposed by the Catholic priest and physics professor Monsignor Georges Lemaître?
- a. Collision theory
- b. Plate tectonics theory
- c. Molecular theory
- d. Germ theory
- e. Big Bang theory

Q259: Name the 17th century Catholic who has been dubbed the "Father of Modern Philosophy" and the "Father of Modern Mathematics."
- a. René Descartes
- b. Alessandro Volta
- c. Galileo Galilei
- d. André-Marie Ampere
- e. Nicolaus Copernicus

Q260: Name the Catholic priest and astronomer who is known as the Father of Heliocentric Cosmology.
- a. René Descartes
- b. Alessandro Volta
- c. Galileo Galilei
- d. André-Marie Ampere
- e. Nicolaus Copernicus

Q261: Which *three* of the following electrical units were named after Catholic physicists?
- a. Volt
- b. Watt
- c. Farad
- d. Coulomb
- e. Ampere

Q262: What electricity-related phenomenon was discovered by an 18th century Catholic physicist after he dissected animals such as frogs?
- a. Lightning
- b. Photoelectric effect
- c. Pyroelectric effect
- d. Galvanism
- e. Static electricity

Q263: Which 17th century invention by the Catholic physicist and mathematician Evangelista Torricelli is still used today by meteorologists around the world?
- a. Calculator
- b. Weather balloon
- c. Barometer
- d. Hygrometer
- e. Weather vane

Q264: Father Roger Joseph Boscovich (1711-1787), a Croatian Jesuit astronomer and mathematician, is credited with groundbreaking work that was a precursor to _____.
- a. Modern atomic theory
- b. Blank slate theory
- c. Aurora borealis
- d. Cold fusion
- e. The Martian canals

A258: (e) The Big Bang Theory. The Big Bang model – widely accepted today – holds that the universe was formed from the explosion of a single infinitely dense and hot point; the universe has been expanding ever since.

A259: (a) René Descartes (1596-1650). This French founder of analytic geometry invented the Cartesian coordinate system – the X,Y system commonly seen in scientific graphs and algebra classes – which was named after him.

A260: (e) Nicolaus Copernicus (1473-1543). This Polish astronomer founded heliocentric planetary theory, providing a scientific basis for a sun-centered solar system. His masterpiece, *De revolutionibus orbium coelestium* ("On the Revolutions of the Celestial Spheres"), shaped the world's understanding of physics and astronomy.

A261: (a, d, e) The volt was named after Alessandro Volta, the coulomb for Charles Augustin de Coulomb, and the ampere for André-Marie Ampere.

A262: (d) Galvanism. Discovered by Luigi Galvani, this phenomenon pertains to muscles contracting when stimulated by an electric current.

A263: (c) Barometer. Torricelli discovered that the rising or lowering of mercury in a glass tube indicated changes in atmospheric pressure.

A264: (a) Modern atomic theory.

Q265: At least 35 of these were named after Jesuit scientists and mathematicians. What are they?
a. Moon craters
b. Stars
c. Galaxies
d. Meteors
e. Comets

Q266: Jesuit physicist Francesco Grimaldi, who discovered the diffraction of light, is known for making a map of what?
a. Ocean floor
b. Surface of the moon
c. Night sky
d. Amazon rainforest
e. Yukon

Q267: What job title has Jesuit astronomer Guy J. Consolmagno, S.J., Ph.D. had since his assignment to the Vatican Observatory in Castel Gondolfo, Italy in 1993?
a. Curator of the Vatican meteorite collection
b. Curator of telescopes
c. Curator of rare species
d. Curator of papal spacecrafts
e. Curator of coral

Q268: The Jesuit astronomer Christopher Clavius was known as the "Euclid of the 16th century," and was known for his mathematical work related to the earth's orbit which assisted in the creation of the _____.
a. First spaceship
b. First compass
c. Gregorian calendar
d. Satellite
e. Ocean maps

Q269: What did Jesuit astronomer and anatomist Christopher Scheiner discover while studying the sun in 1611?
a. Solar eclipse blindness
b. Sunspots
c. Sunblock
d. Helium
e. Hydrogen

A265: (a) Moon craters.

A266: (b) Surface of the moon. Drawn in 1645, Grimaldi's basic map for lunar nomenclature was used for centuries.

A267: (a) Curator of the Vatican meteorite collection, one of the world's largest collections. Dr. Consolmagno is a Jesuit brother, not a priest. He is the author of *Brother Astronomer: Adventures of a Vatican Scientist* and *Turn Left at Orion*.

A268: (c) Gregorian calendar. A friend of Johannes Kepler, Clavius was also the first to use the decimal point and parentheses in mathematics.

A269: (b) The existence of sunspots. Scheiner's other achievements include his proof that the eye's retina was the actual organ of vision.

Q270: Which Catholic chemist conducted experiments that confirmed that diseases were caused by the spread of germs?
a. Sir Alexander Fleming
b. Louis Pasteur
c. Henry Becquerel
d. Roger Bacon
e. Fr. Athanasius Kircher

Q271: Which of these was developed by Catholic biologist Alexander Fleming?
a. Penicillin
b. Steroids
c. Advil
d. Benadryl
e. Allegra

Q272: Gregor Mendel, the Catholic priest and monk who became known as the father of modern genetics, is famous for his studies of inheritance patterns of what?
a. Watermelons
b. Pea plants
c. Grape vines
d. Venus Flytraps
e. Puppies

Q273: Which Catholic French genius helped prove that light travels faster in air than in water, thus overturning a theory defended by Kepler and Newton?
a. León Foucault
b. Marie Curie
c. René Descartes
d. Gregor Mendel
e. Jean Picard

Q274: In 2009, carbon-dating tests on human bone fragments confirmed that the bones dated back to the first or second century. The bones are believed to be those of _____.
a. Pontius Pilate
b. St. Joseph
c. St. Paul the Apostle
d. St. John the Baptist
e. King Herod

A270: (b) Louis Pasteur. Credited with confirming the germ theory of disease and with inventing pasteurization, this 19th century French chemist died with a rosary in his hand. Known as the father of bacteriology, Pasteur is acclaimed for a long list of breakthroughs in disease prevention.

A271: (a) Penicillin. For discovering this antibiotic, Fleming shared the Nobel Prize in Physiology or Medicine in 1945 with Howard Florey and Ernst Chain, who isolated penicillin and made it usable.

A272: (b) Pea plants. Gregor Mendel (1822-1884), an Augustinian priest and monk, made ground-breaking discoveries about the laws that determined inherited traits in pea plants after planting and studying approximately 29,000 plants in his monastery's gardens for eight years.

A273: (a) León Foucault (1819-1868). In a vacuum, the speed of light, or "c," remains constant, but translucent and clear media slow light, with water slowing it down more than air. Foucault, a French physicist, also invented the Foucault pendulum, devised to demonstrate the earth's rotation. Foucault demonstrated his device in 1851 at the Panthéon in Paris.

A274: (c) St. Paul the Apostle. Archeologists had removed the bones from the Apostle's marble sarcophagus under the Basilica of St. Paul's Outside the Walls in Rome. "This seems to confirm the unanimous and uncontested tradition that they are the mortal remains of the Apostle Paul," said Pope Benedict XVI on June 28, 2009.

Q275: Which human body part was discovered in the 16th century by a Catholic physician?
    a. Superior Vena Cava
    b. Duodenum
    c. Spleen
    d. Parathyroid
    e. Fallopian tubes

Q276: What invention by Catholic physician René Laennec in 1816 did he refer to as "the greatest legacy of my life"?
    a. Syringe
    b. Wheelchair
    c. Artificial blood
    d. Ultrasound
    e. Stethoscope

Q277: Which mentor of St. Thomas Aquinas received the title "the Great" for his vast knowledge of almost every field of learning of his time?
    a. Albert the Great
    b. Alexander the Great
    c. Catherine the Great
    d. Frederick the Great
    e. Gregory the Great

Q278: What did Nobel Prize winner and surgeon Alexis Carrel witness at Lourdes in 1903 that contributed to his conversion to Catholicism many years later?
    a. An apparition
    b. Sign in the sky
    c. A pilgrim's instant cure
    d. Nuns in prayer
    e. Kindness

Q279: Father Theodor Wulf (1868-1946) discovered cosmic rays after taking an electrometer to the top of which building?
    a. Leaning Tower of Pisa
    b. Eiffel Tower
    c. Big Ben
    d. Taj Mahal
    e. Burj Khalifa

A275: (e) Fallopian tubes. They were discovered by, and named after Gabriello Fallopio.

A276: (e) Stethoscope. Dr. Laennec, a French physician, invented the tool as a way to spare women (and himself) the embarrassment caused by doctors placing their heads to a patient's chest to listen to the heartbeat.

A277: (a) Albert the Great, also known as St. Albertus Magnus (d. 1280 A.D.). This Dominican friar priest and Doctor of the Church was considered a genius in philosophy, theology, astronomy, chemistry, botany, geography, and other fields. He insisted that each scientific discovery about Creation further revealed the nature of God. His contemporaries dubbed him "Doctor Universalis" (Universal Doctor).

A278: (c) The instantaneous cure of a girl with acute peritonitis at Lourdes, France (site of Church-approved Marian apparitions). Carrel, an agnostic surgeon and biologist who won the Nobel Prize for Physiology or Medicine in 1912, later returned to the Catholic faith of his youth.

A279: (b) Eiffel Tower. A German physicist and Jesuit priest, Fr. Wulf built an electrometer that detected more electromagnetic waves at the top of the tower than at the bottom, thus confirming the presence of radiation originating from outer space.

Chapter Seven
Culture

Q280: Approximately how many Catholics are there in the world today?
a. One million
b. 250 million
c. 500 million
d. 750 million
e. One billion

Q281: Which continent has the highest Catholic population?
a. Europe
b. Asia
c. Africa
d. South America
e. North America

Q282: How many Catholic priests are there around the globe?
a. 5,000+
b. 50,000+
c. 400,000+
d. One million
e. Three million

Q283: In which countries do Catholics *not* make up the majority of the population?
a. Argentina and Brazil
b. France and Portugal
c. Poland and Hungary
d. Canada and Switzerland
e. Austria and Chile

Q284: On which continent is the Catholic population growing the most quickly?
a. Europe
b. Asia
c. Africa
d. South America
e. North America

Q285: What country boasts the highest Catholic population?
a. Brazil
b. Philippines
c. United States
d. Mexico
e. Italy

Q286: In which U.S. state do Catholics comprise more than half of the total population?
a. Rhode Island
b. California
c. Texas
d. Pennsylvania
e. New Jersey

A280: (e) 1.2 billion. Of the 6.3 billion people in the world, more than a billion are Catholics, accounting for more than half of all Christians worldwide.

A281: (d) South America, with 324.3 million Catholics (Our Sunday Visitor's *Catholic Almanac*, 2009).

A282: (c) 412,236 priests, according to a Vatican statistic published in 2012.

A283: (d) Canada (44% Catholic) and Switzerland (46% Catholic).

A284: (c) Africa. Asia ranks second (Our Sunday Visitor's *Catholic Almanac*, 2009).

A285: (a) Brazil has the highest. Mexico, the Philippines, and the United States rank second, third and fourth.

A286: (a) Rhode Island. Massachusetts ranks second with almost half of its population reporting to be Catholic. However, the states with the most Catholic residents total would be California, New York and Texas (Our Sunday Visitor's *Catholic Almanac*, 2009).

Q287: Attended by the pope, which event featured the following lineup: Denver (1993), Toronto (2002), Cologne (2005), Sydney (2008), Madrid (2011) and Rio de Janeiro (2013)?
- a. Catholic Woodstock
- b. Apparition in Lourdes
- c. Election of pope
- d. Pro-life march
- e. World Youth Day

Q288: Which country declared a week of mourning in 2009 after the death of a beloved former president, a devout Catholic who quashed a dictatorship and restored democracy there in the 1980s?
- a. Cuba
- b. South Korea
- c. Slovakia
- d. Poland
- e. Philippines

Q289: On what continent would you find an ice-covered peninsula named after Pope John Paul II?
- a. Antarctica
- b. Asia
- c. South America
- d. Europe
- e. Australia

Q290: In 2008, Col. Ronald Garan brought relics of St. Thérèse of Lisieux to a place they had never gone before. To what location were the relics brought?
- a. Bottom of Pacific Ocean
- b. Bottom of volcano
- c. North Pole
- d. Mount Everest
- e. Outer space

Q291: Which of the Twelve Apostles is believed by historians to have traveled east to preach in India?
- a. St. Andrew
- b. St. Matthew
- c. St. John
- d. St. Thomas
- e. St. Jude

Q292: What is the world's oldest and largest institution?
- a. UNESCO
- b. U.S. government
- c. University of Bologna
- d. City of Jericho
- e. Catholic Church

A287: (e) World Youth Day. Founded in 1984 by Pope John Paul II, the event celebrates the Catholic faith and unity of cultures. The 1995 WYD in Manila, Philippines drew more than 4 million pilgrims, making it one of the largest peaceful gatherings in history.

A288: (e) Philippines. The president was Corazon Aquino (1933-2009). Known as the "Icon of Philippines Democracy," Aquino advocated using peaceful means as she helped restore democracy to her island country when she became president in 1986. Having replaced Dictator Ferdinand Marcos, Aquino was *Time* magazine's "Woman of the Year" for 1986, and was nominated (but did not win) the Nobel Peace Prize in 1986. She was devoted to the rosary, the Mass, and to Our Lady of Fatima.

A289: (a) Antarctica. The Ioannes Paulus II Peninsula is located on the north coast of Livingston Island, Antarctica. The pope received the honor for contributing to world peace.

A290: (e) Outer space. The astronaut placed the relics in orbit around the earth.

A291: (d) St. Thomas. On February 5, 1986, Pope John Paul II visited the site believed to be the Apostle's tomb at the Cathedral Basilica of St. Thomas the Apostle in Madras, India.

A292: (e) The Catholic Church, founded on St. Peter in 32 A.D. by Jesus Christ (Mt 16:18-19), and with a current membership of more than one billion.

Q293: The second Monday of each October, Columbus Day marks the anniversary of Christopher Columbus' discovery of the Americas on October 12, 1492. Where did this Catholic evangelist first hit shore?
- a. Massachusetts
- b. Delaware
- c. Florida
- d. The Bahamas
- e. Canada

Q294: The saint for whom St. Valentine's Day was named was _____.
- a. An early Catholic priest or bishop
- b. A friend of St. Patrick
- c. Not a real person
- d. An explorer
- e. Married three times

Q295: The shamrock is associated with St. Patrick's Day because St. Patrick, the second bishop of Ireland, demonstrated the dogma of _____ using one.
- a. The Incarnation
- b. Transubstantiation
- c. Atonement
- d. Original Sin
- e. The Trinity

Q296: Who ordered St. Patrick to gather the Irish race into the one fold of Christ?
- a. Jesus
- b. St. Peter
- c. St. Paul
- d. Pope Celestine
- e. Bishop Palladius

Q297: Catholic school students can sleep late the morning after Halloween because schools are off on the November 1 feast day known as _____.
- a. All Saints Day
- b. All Souls' Day
- c. The Assumption
- d. The Ascension
- e. Day of the Dead

Q298: In a letter to the Spanish king and queen, what did Christopher Columbus request for his newly discovered islands in the New World?
- a. A shipment of molasses and biscuits
- b. A church and some priests
- c. Bibles in the Native American languages
- d. Relics of St. Peter
- e. Faster postal service

A293: (d) The Bahamas, islands off the southeast coast of Florida. Columbus named the first Bahaman island "San Salvador" (Holy Savior).

A294: (a) An early Catholic priest or bishop. Of the three St. Valentines mentioned in the early Christian Martyrologies under February 14, one is listed as a priest, one as a bishop, and all three as martyrs. Some wonder if all three men are one and the same.

A295: (e) The Trinity. A three-leafed clover, the shamrock has become the symbol of Ireland.

A296: (d) Pope Celestine, in the early 5th century. St. Patrick is known as "the Apostle of Ireland."

A297: (a) All Saints Day, honoring all saints in heaven, known and unknown. November 2 is All Souls' Day, devoted to deceased souls not yet in heaven.

A298: (b) A church and some priests to say Mass and help convert Native Americans. Written in the 1490s, the letter recommends having "a church, and parish priests or friars to administer the sacraments, to perform divine worship, and for the conversion of the Indians."

Q299: The legend of Santa Claus is based on a bearded Catholic bishop from modern-day _____.
   a. Israel
   b. Italy
   c. Lebanon
   d. Greece
   e. Turkey

Q300: From what word or phrase does the word "Christmas" originate?
   a. Christ's Mass
   b. Christ's manger
   c. Jingle Bells
   d. Gift cards
   e. Winter

Q301: The "twelve days" of Christmas begin on Christmas Day and end on January 5. The following day, January 6 marks the _____.
   a. Epiphany
   b. Ascension
   c. Assumption
   d. Presentation
   e. Spy Wednesday

Q302: Which saint is believed to have put together the first nativity scene?
   a. St. Augustine
   b. St. Monica
   c. St. Patrick
   d. St. Christopher
   e. St. Francis of Assisi

A299: (e) Turkey. The name Santa Claus was derived from the name St. Nicholas ("Santa" means "saint." The last half of "Nicholas" sounds like "Claus."). Jolly Old St. Nick was the bearded bishop of Myra in Asia Minor (modern-day Turkey) in the 4th century. He was known for giving gifts and working miracles.

A300: (a) Christ's Mass. So, don't take the Mass out of Christmas! The name "Christmas" has been around since 1038 when it started as the old English "Christes Maesse" and became "crist-messe" by 1131. In many countries, though, the holiday takes the name from the word "birth" (e.g. "Natale" in Italian and "Navidad" in Spanish).

A301: (a) The Epiphany is also known as Three Kings' Day because January 6 is associated with the visit of the Magi (or Wise Men) to the Baby Jesus in Bethlehem (Mt 2:1-12), and thus the manifestation of the glory of Christ to the Gentiles.

A302: (e) St. Francis of Assisi. In his book *The Life of St. Francis of Assisi*, St. Bonaventure writes that St. Francis, with the pope's permission, "prepared a manger, and brought hay, and an ox and an ass," then stood before the scene "bathed in tears and radiant with joy" and began preaching the Gospel.

Q303: Which of these artists was not a Catholic?
    a. Michelangelo   d. Rembrandt
    b. Leonardo da Vinci   e. Andy Warhol
    c. Raphael

Q304: Which was not created by a Catholic?
    a. Statues entitled *David* and *Pietà*   d. *The Last Supper*
    b. *The Birth of Venus*   e. *Mona Lisa*
    c. *Return of the Prodigal Son*

Q305: Which great Italian painter created sketches and plans for a helicopter, tank, calculator, solar power, and the double hull centuries before they were introduced to the world?
    a. Michelangelo   d. Botticelli
    b. Leonardo da Vinci   e. Donatello
    c. Raphael

Q306: Which country is home to a famous painting of the Virgin Mary with the Christ Child that was believed to have been painted by St. Luke, author of the third Gospel?
    a. Israel   d. Poland
    b. Greece   e. Italy
    c. Syria

Q307: In 1854, Pope Pius IX donated a marble block for the construction of a U.S. building. Which building?
    a. The Washington Monument   d. The White House
    b. Union Station   e. The U.S. Supreme Court
    c. The Pentagon

Q308: After centuries of never leaving the Vatican, Michelangelo's *Pietà* went on a trip in 1964 to appear at an event thousands of miles away. To which city did it travel?
    a. Washington, D.C., for the Inauguration of U.S. President Lyndon B. Johnson
    b. Washington, D.C., for the founding of Peace Corps
    c. New York, for the World's Fair
    d. Los Angeles, for the first Super Bowl
    e. Bethel, N.Y., for the Woodstock concert

A303: (d) Rembrandt. Known as the greatest Protestant artist, Rembrandt van Rijn was a Dutch 17th century painter of landscapes and portraits, including images of apostles, saints, monks, the Virgin Mary, and Christ.

A304: (c) *Return of the Prodigal Son* (by Rembrandt). Leonardo da Vinci painted *The Last Supper* and the *Mona Lisa*. Michelangelo sculpted the *Pietà* and *David*. Michelangelo also painted the fresco entitled *Creation of Adam* on the ceiling of the Sistine Chapel. Sandro Botticelli painted *The Birth of Venus*.

A305: (b) Leonardo da Vinci (1452-1519). This archetype of the "Renaissance Man" was not only one of history's greatest painters, but also was an engineer, mathematician, inventor, botanist, architect, musician, and writer.

A306: (d) Poland. The painting, known as the Black Madonna of Częstochowa, is Poland's holiest relic and has been visited by Pope John Paul II. Credited with many miracles, Our Lady of Częstochowa was reportedly seen by many witnesses appearing in the clouds above Warsaw on September 14, 1920 as a sign of her protection as the Russian army prepared to attack. The subsequent Polish victory is known as the Miracle of Vistula.

A307: (a) The Washington Monument, in Washington, D.C. The obelisk is one of the world's tallest stone structures. Sadly, before it could be used, the donated "Pope's Stone" was stolen by masked thieves, who were assumed to have thrown it into the nearby Potomac River. The men were identified as members of the "Know-Nothing" Party, an anti-Catholic and anti-immigrant group. A replica of the original pope's stone was dedicated at the Washington Monument in 1982.

A308: (c) The New York World's Fair. Pope John XXIII gave permission for the lending of the *Pietà*, a marble sculpture portraying the Body of Christ in His mother's arms. The masterpiece was returned safely to St. Peter's Basilica in Vatican City. In 1965, Pope Paul VI banned the loaning of art from the Vatican.

Q309: Which pair of composers was not Catholic?
a. Beethoven and Mozart
b. Schubert and Palestrina
c. Bach and Handel
d. Vivaldi and Verdi
e. Haydn and Liszt

Q310: Antonio Vivaldi, a Catholic priest from Venice, wrote a famous set of four violin concertos in the Baroque style celebrating _____.
a. Matthew, Mark, Luke and John
b. Peter, Paul, Mary, and Joseph
c. Gold, silver, frankincense and myrrh
d. Spring, summer, fall and winter
e. Leonardo, Donatello, Raphael, Michelangelo

Q311: A Catholic monk named Guido of Arezzo is regarded as the inventor of:
a. Classical music
b. Musical notation
c. Singing waitresses
d. The conductor's wand
e. Gregorian Chant

Q312: Which of the following has Catholic composer Franz Joseph Haydn *not* been hailed as?
a. Inventor of the symphony
b. Father of instrumentation
c. Creator of modern chamber music
d. Founder of the Viennese school of composition
e. Founder of Latin-language music

Q313: In what city would you find the Catholic church in which the great piano composer Frédéric Chopin's heart is buried?
a. Hamburg
b. Brussels
c. Warsaw
d. Prague
e. St. Petersburg

A309: (c) Johann Sebastian Bach (1685-1750), a German composer and organist, and Georg Friedrich Handel (1685-1759), best known for his famous oratorio *The Messiah* (with its *Hallelujah Chorus*), were Lutherans.

A310: (d) *The Four Seasons* is the best-known work of Antonio Vivaldi (1678-1741). It was in 1723 that he composed its four parts, entitled "Spring," "Summer," "Fall," and "Winter," each resembling its respective sounds of nature.

A311: (b) Musical notation or staff notation. Guido of Arezzo (d. 1050 A.D.) was a monk of the Order of St. Benedict.

A312: (e) He was *not* the founder of Latin-language music. An Austrian composer, Haydn lived from 1732 to 1809.

A313: (c) Warsaw, Poland. The heart of Chopin (1810-1849) is buried at Holy Cross Church.

Q314: Which of these books was not written by a Catholic?
    a. *Chronicles of Narnia*   d. *Democracy in America*
    b. *The Lord of the Rings*   e. *Don Quixote*
    c. *The Canterbury Tales*

Q315: The European Union has three official alphabets. Which one was invented by a Catholic saint in the ninth century?
    a. The Greek alphabet   d. The Arabic alphabet
    b. The Roman alphabet   e. The Georgian alphabet
    c. The Cyrillic alphabet

Q316: A French priest named Charles-Michel de l'Épée (1712-1789) is known as the "Father of the _____" while a Spanish priest named Juan Pablo Bonet (1573-1633) was an earlier pioneer in the education of the _____.
    a. Blind   d. Physically impaired
    b. Deaf   e. Paralyzed
    c. Mentally challenged

Q317: Name the printing technique invented by Aloys Senefelder in 1796.
    a. Woodblock printing   d. Lithography
    b. Moveable type   e. Linotype
    c. Mimeograph

Q318: What language is spoken by more Catholics today than any other language?
    a. Chinese   d. Spanish
    b. French   e. English
    c. Russian

Q319: Father Brown was the best-known character created by what Anglican-turned-Catholic writer from England?
    a. Charles II of England   d. Dorothy Day
    b. John Henry Newman   e. G.K. Chesterton
    c. Richard Crashaw

A314: (a) *Chronicles of Narnia*. Its Anglican author, C.S. Lewis (1898-1963), a former atheist and friend of J.R.R. Tolkien, also wrote the Christian apologetics classic, *Mere Christianity*. The other books have Catholic authors: *The Lord of the Rings* (J.R.R. Tolkien), *The Canterbury Tales* (Chaucer), *Democracy in America* (Alexis de Tocqueville), and *Don Quixote* (Cervantes).

A315: (c) The Cyrillic alphabet – invented by St. Cyril – is used by Slavic languages such as Russian, Serbian, and Bulgarian, and non-Slavic ones such as Mongolian. When Bulgaria joined the European Union in January 2007, the Cyrillic alphabet became the E.U.'s third official alphabet (after Latin and Greek). St. Cyril and his brother, St. Methodius, both priests and monks born in Thessaloniki, Greece, are known as the Apostles of the Slavs.

A316: (b) Deaf. Épée opened the first free school for the deaf; his method for teaching sign language was imitated around the world. Bonet wrote the first book on deaf education in 1620.

A317: (d) Lithography. Senefelder, an Austrian actor, invented this printing technique in 1796, thus paving the way for the development of modern holy cards.

A318: (d) Spanish.

A319: (e) G.K. Chesterton (1874-1936) used the priest detective character in short stories. The author of novels such as *The Man Who Was Thursday*, Chesterton would debate atheists such as playwright George Bernard Shaw.

Q320: Often listed as one of the 100 best English-language novels of the 20th century, *Death Comes for the Archbishop* (1927) follows the attempts of a Catholic bishop and a priest to found a diocese in what new U.S. territory?
- a. Florida
- b. New Mexico
- c. Alaska
- d. California
- d. Texas

Q321: Who is called the "Father of the Italian Language"?
- a. Chaucer
- b. Shakespeare
- c. Manzoni
- d. Carducci
- e. Dante

Q322: In Iraq, some Masses are still said in _____, the native language of Jesus.
- a. Hebrew
- b. Latin
- c. Arabic
- d. Aramaic
- e. Armenian

Q323: Which would not be a language in which Mass was celebrated in very early Christianity?
- a. Aramaic
- b. Hebrew
- c. Greek
- d. Latin
- e. Quechua

Q324: Who authored *Jesus of Nazareth*, which had sales of two million copies in the first six months after its 2007 release?
- a. Anne Rice
- b. William F. Buckley, Jr.
- c. Flannery O'Connor
- d. Alexander Pope
- e. Pope Benedict XVI

Q325: Name the late British journalist, author and satirist who is known as the "discoverer of Mother Teresa."
- a. Malcolm Muggeridge
- b. Oscar Wilde
- c. Hilaire Belloc
- d. John Dryden
- e. Laura Ingraham

A320: (b) New Mexico. Willa Cather wrote the novel.

A321: (e) Dante Alighieri (1265-1321). This Italian poet's masterpiece was the *Divina Commedia* (Divine Comedy), an imaginary journey through hell, purgatory and paradise.

A322: (d) Aramaic was the everyday language of Jesus and of Palestine in the first century. Jesus would have also spoken Greek – the language of trade – and Hebrew.

A323: (e) Quechua.

A324: (e) Pope Benedict XVI.

A325: (a) Malcolm Muggeridge (1903-1990), whose first interview with the little nun in 1968 aired on BBC. This led to a five-day shoot in Calcutta in 1969, producing the acclaimed documentary, *Something Beautiful for God*, revealing the humanitarian work of Mother Teresa. Later, Muggeridge wrote a book of the same title. In 1982, Muggeridge and his wife became Catholic.

Q326: Which business was founded in 1960 by a man who is now a devout Catholic philanthropist?
    a. Starbucks   d. Subway
    b. Domino's Pizza   e. Cheesecake Factory
    c. Applebee's

Q327: What food, once forbidden during Lent, was brought to the table on Easter Day to symbolize the joy of the Resurrection?
    a. Chocolate   d. Pudding
    b. Lamb   e. Ice cream
    c. Eggs

Q328: By which name is Norma McCorvey better known?
    a. Jane Roe   d. Mother Teresa
    b. Jane Doe   e. Hannah Montana
    c. Grace Kelly

Q329: By what name is Rob Evans, a popular children's evangelist who became Catholic in 2006, better known as?
    a. The Donut Man   d. The Twizzler Man
    b. The Lego Man   e. Jack the Bulldog
    c. The Pie Man

Q330: Originally bred for alpine rescues, what breed of working dog from the Swiss Alps was named after an 11th century monk and priest?
    a. Appenzell Mountain Dog   d. Weimaraner
    b. Beauceron   e. St. Bernard
    c. Komondor

Q331: Which of the following people did not convert to the Catholic Church?
    a. Newt Gingrich   d. Bob Hope
    b. Tony Blair   e. Jeb Bush
    c. William F. Buckley, Jr.

Q332: Which star of the former ABC television series, *Fantasy Island*, was made a Knight Commander of St. Gregory the Great in 1998 by Pope John Paul II?
    a. Hervé Villechaize   d. Gavin MacLeod
    b. Ricardo Montalbán   e. Fred Grandy
    c. Christopher Hewett

A326: (b) Domino's Pizza. Founder Thomas Monaghan sold Domino's in 1998, and has since invested hundreds of millions of dollars in charitable, religious and pro-life causes.

A327: (c) Eggs. According to the original *Catholic Encyclopedia*, the eggs were often colored red to symbolize the Easter joy.

A328: (a) Jane Roe (of Roe vs. Wade, the infamous court case of 1973 that legalized abortion in all 50 states). Roe, who was the lead plaintiff in the case, has since undergone a change of heart and now works as a pro-life activist. In 1995, she was baptized by an evangelical Protestant minister, and in 1998, after three years of prayer, she announced her decision to enter the Catholic Church.

A329: (a) The Donut Man. Rob Evans' alter ego, the "Donut Man," has been Evans' full time ministry for more than 20 years. A former evangelical Protestant, Evans hosts children's concerts and videos, belting out lyrics such as: "Life without Jesus is like a donut; there's a hole in the middle of your heart."

A330: (e) The St. Bernard dog was ultimately named after St. Bernard of Menthon, who was born in France in 923 A.D. The dogs populated the area of the Great St. Bernard Pass through the Alps and the Great St. Bernard Hospice for travelers. Both were named after St. Bernard, now patron of the Alps. The dog also acquired the saint's name as the hospice used the dogs to rescue travelers trapped in deep snow.

A331: (c) William F. Buckley, Jr. (1925-2008) grew up Catholic, as did his ten brothers and sisters.

A332: (b) Ricardo Montalbán (1920-2009). Born in Mexico City, Montalbán played Mr. Roarke on *Fantasy Island* from 1978-1984. His television sidekick, Tatoo, was played by Hervé Villechaize. Montalbán has said his Catholic faith was the most important thing in his life.

Q333: Name the member of The Three Tenors who released a CD in late 2008 with songs inspired by poems by Pope John Paul II?
- a. Luciano Pavarotti
- b. José Carreras
- c. Plácido Domingo
- d. Mario Dradi
- e. Andrea Bocelli

Q334: Completed in 1931, which famous landmark was built by John J. Raskob, who had been named a Knight of the Order of St. Gregory the Great by Pope Pius XI?
- a. Leaning Tower of Pisa
- b. Empire State Building
- c. Golden Gate Bridge
- d. St. Patrick's Cathedral
- e. Jefferson Memorial

Q335: What is Theology of the Body?
- a. A ground-breaking Scriptural analysis by Pope John Paul II regarding the unity of mind, body and spirit
- b. A theory about the qualities of human bodies in heaven
- c. A doctrine concerning hospitals and surgery
- d. A doctrine about athletic pursuits
- e. A theory that thin people are less likely to go to heaven

Q336: To what does Theology on Tap refer?
- a. The flow of religious prayer on the Internet
- b. A secret ceremony for tapping future priests for ordination
- c. Theology lectures in a pub; religion plus cheese steaks, burgers and beer
- d. Theologians playing basketball
- e. Tap dancing while teaching CCD

Q337: What Catholic newspaper, still in circulation today, was founded on May 5, 1912 to counter misinformation from anti-Catholic publications?
- a. *National Catholic Register*
- b. *Our Sunday Visitor*
- c. *Catholic Digest*
- d. *Inside the Vatican*
- e. *Catholic News Service*

Q338: In which United States city would you find the Knights of Columbus Museum?
- a. Columbia, SC
- b. Columbus, OH
- c. New Haven, CT
- d. Newport, RI
- e. Milwaukee, WI

A333: (c) Plácido Domingo. His CD was entitled "Amore Infinito" (Italian for "Infinite Love"). Domingo, José Carreras and the late Luciano Pavarotti were The Three Tenors.

A334: (b) Empire State Building. Raskob (1879-1950) served as Chair of the Democratic National Committee and as an executive of the DuPont chemical company and General Motors. He established several non-profit Catholic foundations.

A335: (a) A ground-breaking Scriptural analysis by Pope John Paul II on God's design for human sexuality, marriage, virginity, purity, celibacy, the resurrection of the body, human love and freedom, and the spousal relationship between Christ and His Church. The work is contained in 129 papal lectures from 1979 to 1984.

A336: (c) Theology lectures in a pub or restaurant attended by Catholic young adults. Founded by a priest in Illinois in 1981, Theology on Tap can be found at parishes all over the United States and in other countries. Scholars and notable speakers – even four cardinals – have been invited to discuss hot topics in religion and morality.

A337: (b) *Our Sunday Visitor*, based in Huntingdon, Indiana. Founded by Fr. (later Bishop) John Noll, this newsweekly had reached a circulation of a million by 1961.

A338: (c) New Haven, Connecticut is home to both the museum and headquarters of the Knights of Columbus, founded in 1882 by Fr. Michael J. McGivney. The museum collection includes artifacts brought to America by Christopher Columbus on his second voyage in 1493. The Knights boast about 1.7 million members.

Q339: At seven monasteries in Belgium, monks produce _____ to generate revenues to help pay the monastery's bills.
    a. Wigs
    b. Leather boots
    c. Christmas trees
    d. Bibles
    e. Beer

Q340: One common legend about the origin of the world's oldest snack food, is that monks in southern France made them in 610 A.D. using dough left over from bread making. Name the snack food.
    a. Funnel cake
    b. Pretzels
    c. Tortillas
    d. Scones
    e. Elephant Ears

Q341: Which one of the following groups is a Catholic forbidden from joining?
    a. Opus Dei
    b. Masons
    c. Augustinians
    d. Franciscans
    e. Knights of Columbus

Q342: The modern Gregorian calendar, named after Pope Gregory XIII, replaced the Julian calendar, named after _____.
    a. Juliana of Norwich
    b. Pope Julius III
    c. Julius Africanus
    d. Julius Caesar
    e. Julian the Apostate

Q343: Which bird got its name from a Catholic Church official?
    a. Quail
    b. Hawk
    c. Eagle
    d. Swan
    e. Cardinal

A339: (e) Beer. Trappist monks in Belgium produce top-ranking beers such as Westvleteren, Chimay, Rochefort, Achel, Orval, Westmalle and La Trappe (Koningshoeven). However, most Trappist monks and nuns around the globe are *not* in the brewing business.

A340: (b) Pretzels. Known as the bread of Lent, the first pretzels emerged at a time strict Lenten fasting required abstinence from not only meat, but also milk, cheese, butter and eggs. According to one legend, a monk folded bread dough in the shape of crossed arms in prayer to make the first pretzel.

A341: (b) The Masons. The Church regards multiple tenets of Freemasonry incompatible with Christianity, including the belief in a vague god (the Grand Architect of the Universe) and the idea that we may be saved by our good works, independent of God's grace.

A342: (d) Julius Caesar, Roman dictator and conqueror of Gaul who reigned from 49 to 44 B.C. Decreed in 1582, the Gregorian calendar reformed the Julian calendar, which had lost more than nine days between the 1st and 16th centuries. The Gregorian calendar corrected this loss, but now October 4 was followed by October 15. Unlike the Julian calendar, the Gregorian calendar omits three leap days every 400 years.

A343: (e) Cardinal. This red bird was named for the red vestments worn by cardinals, who are Church officials usually selected from among the world's bishops. The College of Cardinals elects the pope.

Q344: Starring Robert De Niro, *The Mission* features a scene of a Jesuit missionary priest bound to a cross, which is tossed over the edge of scenic _____ by Iguazu Indians.

    a. Machu Picchu   d. Iguazu Falls
    b. Tierra del Fuego   e. Aconcagua
    c. Angel Falls

Q345: Name the Oscar-winning 1943 Hollywood movie which told the story of Church-approved apparitions to a French saint.

    a. *The Bells of St. Mary's*   d. *Lilies of the Field*
    b. *Joan of Arc*   e. *The Song of Bernadette*
    c. *Thérèse*

Q346: What reason or reasons did the director of *The Passion of the Christ* give for choosing actor Jim Caviezel to play the role of Jesus Christ (besides his acting skills)?

    a. The actor was born in Bethlehem
    b. The actor was a priest
    c. The actor spoke Aramaic
    d. The actor had suffered much
    e. The actor was 33 and had the same initials as Jesus Christ

Q347: In 2009, it was announced that Hollywood screenwriter Joe Eszterhas – who had undergone a conversion to Christ years *after* writing unchristian films such as *Basic Instinct* and *Showgirls* – would write a film about _____.

    a. The Dead Sea Scrolls
    b. The Second Coming
    c. Our Lady of Guadalupe
    d. St. Paul's shipwreck
    e. The conversion of Jane Roe

Q348: Which of his acting roles does Sir Alec Guinness (1914-2000) credit with his conversion to Catholicism?

    a. Fagin in *Oliver Twist*
    b. Obi-Wan Kenobi in *Star Wars*
    c. Yevgraf in *Doctor Zhivago*
    d. Herbert Pocket in *Great Expectations*
    e. The priest in *Father Brown*

A344: (d) Iguazu Falls. *The Mission* tells the story of a priest in the 1750s who sets up a mission in a South American jungle to convert Guaraní Indians to Christianity. The 1986 British film won an Academy Award for Best Cinematography.

A345: (e) *The Song of Bernadette*. The Virgin Mary appeared to St. Bernadette Soubirous at Lourdes, France in 1858.

A346: (e) The actor was 33, the age of Jesus at His death, and had the initials, J.C.

A347: (c) Our Lady of Guadalupe. Eszterhas, who moved to Ohio, has said he turned to God in 2001 while suffering from throat cancer. Eszterhas thanked God for curing him from cancer in his 2008 book, *Crossbearer: A Memoir of Faith*.

A348: (e) The priest in *Father Brown*. Received into the Catholic Church in 1954, the English actor describes his conversion in his autobiography, *Blessings in Disguise*. His role in *The Bridge on the River Kwai* earned him an Academy Award for Best Actor.

Q349: What is the largest church in Europe?
    a. Cadiz Cathedral
    b. St. Peter's Basilica
    c. San Marco Basilica
    d. Cologne Cathedral
    e. Wawel Cathedral

Q350: Where is the largest basilica outside Rome?
    a. Ivory Coast
    b. New Zealand
    c. Belize
    d. Egypt
    e. Austria

Q351: What is the name of the cathedral church of Rome?
    a. St. John Lateran
    b. St. Clement
    c. Santa Maria Maggiore
    d. Santi Quattro Coronati
    e. St. Peter's

Q352: Where is the largest Catholic cathedral in the world?
    a. Lourdes, France
    b. Guadalajara, Mexico
    c. Florence, Italy
    d. Seville, Spain
    e. Montreal, Canada

Q353: What does Notre Dame mean in French?
    a. Our Nuns
    b. College of Angels
    c. Virgin Martyrs
    d. Our Lady
    e. Nostradamus

Q354: How long did it take to construct Il Duomo di Milano (Milan Cathedral), which is the seat of the Archbishop of Milan?
    a. 50 years
    b. 100 years
    c. Two centuries
    d. Four centuries
    e. Six centuries

Q355: The Basilica of St. John Lateran is all of the following except for one. Which one?
    a. The cathedral church in Rome
    b. The oldest basilica in Rome
    c. The official seat of the Bishop of Rome (pope)
    d. A former synagogue
    e. Mother church of the entire Catholic Church

A349: (b) St. Peter's Basilica in Rome. Some mistakenly believe this basilica to be a cathedral (seat of a bishop), but it is not.

A350: (a) Ivory Coast. The Basilica of Our Lady of Peace is located in Yamoussoukro, Ivory Coast, and was listed as the world's largest church by Guinness World Records when it was completed in 1990, beating out St. Peter's Basilica, which it resembles. Neither St. Peter's nor Our Lady of Peace serves as a cathedral. The largest *cathedral* in the world is Manhattan's Cathedral Church of St. John the Divine, which is the seat of an Episcopal bishop.

A351: (a) The Basilica of St. John Lateran. As the cathedral church of Rome, this basilica is the official seat of the bishop of Rome, or pope. Not all basilicas serve as cathedrals.

A352: (d) Seville, Spain. The Cathedral of Seville is also the world's largest Gothic church.

A353: (d) Our Lady.

A354: (e) Six centuries.

A355: (d) It is not a former synagogue.

Q356: Christians have long believed the Holy House of _____ to be the house where Mary and Joseph raised Jesus in Nazareth, and where the Incarnation took place.
    a. Loreto
    b. Beretta
    c. Staccato
    d. Falsetto
    e. Olives

Q357: Which of the following events did not take place at the Cathedral of Notre Dame in Paris?
    a. Funeral Mass of Charles de Gaulle
    b. Canonization of Joan of Arc
    c. Signing of the Magna Carta
    d. Crowning of Napoleon as Emperor of France
    e. Wedding of Henry of Navarre

Q358: The tallest church in South America is the Cathedral of Maringá in Maringá, Brazil. What inspired its conical design?
    a. Soviet sputnik satellites
    b. Ice cream cones
    c. Papal hats
    d. Washington Monument
    e. Wine bottle

Q359: Name the largest Catholic cathedral in England.
    a. Westminster Cathedral
    b. Lancaster Cathedral
    c. Cathedral of St. Mary
    d. Northampton Cathedral
    e. Leeds Cathedral

Q360: Where is the largest church in the United States?
    a. New York
    b. Washington, D.C.
    c. Miami
    d. Los Angeles
    e. Pittsburgh

Q361: In which South American country is the world's second largest basilica?
    a. Argentina
    b. Brazil
    c. Peru
    d. Chile
    e. Venezuela

Q362: La Sagrada Familia in Barcelona, Spain, will be the tallest church and basilica in the world if it is ever completed. Name the architect who designed it.
    a. Antonio Gaudí
    b. Ricardo Bofill
    c. Santiago Calatrava
    d. Alonzo Cano
    e. Alejandro Zaera

A356: (a) Loreto. Visited by millions and surrounded by a basilica, this tiny stone house is in Loreto, Italy, and is said to have been transported miraculously from Nazareth by angels.

A357: (c) Signing of the Magna Carta. This historic document, which strongly influenced the development of the American Constitution, was signed at Runnymede in England in 1215.

A358: (a) Soviet sputnik satellites.

A359: (a) Westminster Cathedral. This mother church of the Catholic community in England is not to be confused with Westminster Abbey of the Church of England.

A360: (b) Washington, D.C. The country's largest church is the Basilica of the National Shrine of the Immaculate Conception in Washington, D.C.

A361: (b) Brazil. The world's second largest church is the Basilica of the National Shrine of Our Lady of Aparecida, located in Aparecida, Brazil.

A362: (a) Antonio Gaudí. Construction on the popular Spanish attraction began in 1882. The late Antonio Gaudí, its original designer, worked on the church for 40 years. Plans call for a height of 564 feet and completion in 2026.

Q363: Which of the original members of *Saturday Night Live* has a sister who is a Dominican nun?
  a. Dan Aykroyd
  b. John Belushi
  c. Bill Murray
  d. Chevy Chase
  e. Gilda Radner

Q364: Name the Emmy-winning American actor who borrowed his stage name from a Catholic archbishop and theologian whom he admired.
  a. Nicolas Cage
  b. Anthony Quinn
  c. Cary Grant
  d. Jimmy Dean
  e. Martin Sheen

Q365: Name the Emmy Award winner who is regarded as America's first television preacher of significance.
  a. Billy Graham
  b. Mother Angelica
  c. Joel Osteen
  d. Fulton Sheen
  e. Jim Bakker

Q366: Which Academy Award-winning actor – who was ranked 13th on the list of "greatest male stars of all time" by the American Film Institute in 1999 – was baptized a Catholic two days before his 1979 death?
  a. Gregory Peck
  b. John Voigt
  c. John Wayne
  d. Mickey Rourke
  e. Spencer Tracy

Q367: Name the Irish playwright and novelist who was baptized and received into the Catholic Church on his deathbed in 1900.
  a. Samuel Beckett
  b. James Joyce
  c. Oscar Wilde
  d. George Bernard Shaw
  e. William Butler Yeats

A363: (c) Bill Murray. Sister Nancy Murray, O.P., made headlines in recent years for portraying St. Catherine of Siena in a one-woman show.

A364: (e) Martin Sheen. Born Ramón Gerardo Antonio Estévez, Sheen took his stage name in honor of Archbishop Fulton J. Sheen (1895-1979). Martin Sheen, married for more than 50 years, is best known for playing Captain Willard in the film, *Apocalypse Now* and President Josiah Bartlett on the TV drama series, *The West Wing*. He later starred in *The Way*, a 2010 film about a pilgrimage to Santiago, Spain, that was directed by his son, Emilio Estevez.

A365: (d) The late Archbishop Fulton J. Sheen. This bishop of Rochester authored about 90 books and hosted the TV shows *Life is Worth Living* in the early 1950s and *The Fulton Sheen Program* in the 1960s. Despite competing prime time shows starring Milton Berle and Frank Sinatra, Sheen's *Life is Worth Living* held its own. Berle and the archbishop maintained a friendly rivalry, sometimes jesting about the other on air. The theologian graciously received his Emmy in 1952, saying: "I feel it is time I pay tribute to my four writers – Matthew, Mark, Luke and John." Sheen is being considered for sainthood.

A366: (c) John Wayne (1901-1979).

A367: (c) Oscar Wilde. During his life, he had told friends, "Catholicism is the only religion to die in," according to his biographer, Richard Ellmann.

Q368: Six months before he became Catholic, British Prime Minister Tony Blair visited Pope Benedict XVI on June 23, 2007. What gift did Blair present to the pontiff?
- a. A Tudor rose
- b. An honorary degree from Oxford University
- c. A statue of an English pope
- d. Pictures of a famous English convert to Catholicism
- e. An oak tree

Q369: Name the English lawyer who was called the "greatest historical character in English history" by writer G.K. Chesterton and the "person of the greatest virtue this kingdom ever produced" by Jonathan Swift.
- a. Oliver Cromwell
- b. Sir Thomas More
- c. Thomas Aquinas
- d. Winston Churchill
- e. Sir Francis Drake

Q370: Name the Englishman whose story is told in a play and a film entitled *A Man for All Seasons* and who coined the word "utopia" in his book, *Utopia*.
- a. Oliver Cromwell
- b. Sir Thomas More
- c. Thomas Aquinas
- d. Winston Churchill
- e. Sir Francis Drake

Q371: *The Canterbury Tales* by Geoffrey Chaucer feature tales told by pilgrims on their way to the shrine of which English saint and martyr at Canterbury Cathedral?
- a. St. Thomas Becket
- b. St. Simon Stock
- c. St. John Twenge
- d. St. William of York
- e. St. Hugh of Lincoln

A368: (d) Signed pictures of Blessed John Henry Cardinal Newman, C.O. (1801-1890). Newman was an English convert to Catholicism whose masterpieces include *An Essay on the Development of Christian Doctrine, The Idea of a University, A Grammar of Assent,* and *Apologia pro Vita Sua.* This former Anglican priest became Catholic, and eventually a cardinal, after extensive research that proved to him that only the Catholic Church could claim its doctrines developed consistently since the first century. Blair's papal visit occurred on June 23, 2007, his term as prime minister ended on June 27, 2007, and his entrance into the Catholic Church was announced on December 22, 2007.

A369: (b) Sir Thomas More. This Catholic English saint was beheaded in 1535 after refusing to accept the authority of King Henry VIII as the supreme head of the Church of England after the king broke ties with the pope. Henry VIII severed ties after the pope would not grant him an annulment of his marriage to Catherine of Aragon, who had not given him a male heir.

A370: (b) Sir Thomas More.

A371: (a) St. Thomas Becket (c. 1118-1170) was Archbishop of Canterbury before being murdered by the knights of King Henry II. The following year, Henry II "did public penance, and was scourged at the archbishop's tomb."*

* www.newadvent.org/cathen/14676a.htm

Q372: What famous Italian inventor set up Vatican Radio in 1931 for the pope?
- a. Enrico Fermi
- b. Alessandro Volta
- c. Guglielmo Marconi
- d. Nikola Tesla
- e. Evangelista Torricelli

Q373: In 1981, the world's largest Catholic television broadcast station was founded. Name the station.
- a. EWTN
- b. Catholic TV
- c. Sky TV
- d. Family Channel
- e. RealCatholicTV

Q374: Who founded Catholic Answers, the most recognized name today among Catholic apologetics organizations in North America?
- a. Karl Keating
- b. Benedict Groeschel
- c. Mitch Pacwa
- d. Dave Armstrong
- e. Sister Rosalind Moss

Q375: Name the former Presbyterian minister and father of six who is often considered the most widely known Catholic layman in America today.
- a. Dr. Alan Schreck
- b. Dr. Scott Hahn
- c. Patrick Madrid
- d. Jimmy Akin
- e. Mark Shea

Q376: For what achievement was Efren Peñaflorida, a Catholic layman, named the 2009 CNN Hero of the Year?
- a. Building a hospital in Cuba
- b. Feeding hurricane victims in Malaysia
- c. Educating poor kids in the Philippines
- d. Visiting prisoners in El Salvador
- e. Environmental measures

A372: (c) Guglielmo Marconi, the inventor of the radiotelegraph system. On launch day – February 12, 1931 – Nobel Prize winner Marconi kissed the pope's ring and announced that "Pope Pius XI will inaugurate the Radio Station of the Vatican City State. The electric radio waves will transport to all the world his words of peace and blessing... With the help of Almighty God, who allows the many mysterious forces of nature to be used by man, I have been able to prepare this instrument which will accord to the Faithful of all the world the consolation of hearing the voice of the Holy Father..."

A373: (a) EWTN, founded by Mother Angelica. Launched in 1981, EWTN (Eternal Word Television Network) is based in Irondale, Alabama, and is available in 104 million television households in 110 countries.

A374: (a) Karl Keating. He founded Catholic Answers (www.catholic.com) in San Diego in 1979 in response to anti-Catholic propaganda tracts left on cars parked outside Mass.

A375: (b) Dr. Scott Hahn has been called "Luther in reverse." The author of *Rome Sweet Home* and *The Lamb's Supper*, Dr. Hahn is a theology professor at Franciscan University of Steubenville and is the founder and president of the St. Paul Center for Biblical Theology.

A376: (c) To deliver education to poor children, Peñaflorida, 28, started a "push-cart classroom" in Filipino slums where gang membership among the young was prevalent. Peñaflorida's enterprise, called Dynamic Team Company, boasts 10,000 members who have taught 1,500 children to read and write.

Q377: What historic 14-foot-long relic is housed at the Turin Cathedral in Italy?
- a. The manger Jesus was born in
- b. The True Cross
- c. The table used at the Last Supper
- d. The cloth that covered Jesus' body in His tomb
- e. Mural from St. Peter's house

Q378: Name the path in Jerusalem that is thought to have been walked by Jesus on the way to His Crucifixion.
- a. Via Dolorosa
- b. Strada Santa
- c. Scala Santa
- d. Via Media
- e. Via Crucis

Q379: Where is the Church of the Holy Sepulchre, which is believed to be the site of Jesus' burial and Resurrection?
- a. Haifa
- b. Tel Aviv
- c. Jerusalem
- d. Bethlehem
- e. Nazareth

Q380: Whose mother had a church built over the site believed to be the place of Jesus' birth?
- a. Emperor Constantine's
- b. The Apostle John's
- c. St. Augustine's
- d. St. Patrick's
- e. Augustus Caesar's

A377: (d) The Shroud of Turin or piece of linen cloth bearing the image of a crucified man is reputed to be the cloth that covered Jesus in His tomb.

A378: (a) Via Dolorosa, Latin for "Way of Grief." Pilgrims walk this holy path, which is marked by nine Stations of the Cross. The last five of the 14 Stations are inside the church at the end of the route.

A379: (c) Jerusalem. The church is believed to be on the grounds of the Hill of Calvary, or Golgotha, site of the Lord's Crucifixion.

A380: (a) Emperor Constantine's mother, St. Helena, had a church built at the location in the early 300s but Emperor Justinian I later rebuilt it in the 6th century. The Church of the Nativity in Bethlehem is one of the world's oldest churches still in use. It is believed to be built over a cave that formed the stable where Jesus was born in a manger.

Q381: What job in Vatican City would require you to be at least 5'9" tall, single, male, and Catholic?
   a. Lifeguard
   b. Popemobile driver
   c. Swiss Guard
   d. Chapel painter
   e. Tax collector

Q382: In what language are commands given in the Swiss Guard?
   a. English
   b. Italian
   c. French
   d. German
   e. Latin

Q383: From which country must Swiss Guards have citizenship?
   a. England
   b. Switzerland
   c. Sweden
   d. Italy
   e. Any country in Europe

Q384: New recruits of the Swiss Guard are sworn in on May 6 each year because the date commemorates:
   a. The Sack of Rome
   b. End of the Cold War
   c. End of the Second Vatican Council
   d. The encyclical *Humanae Vitae*
   e. The death of Mother Teresa

A381: (c) The Swiss Guard. The Corps of the Pontifical Swiss Guard, founded in 1506, is the army of Vatican City. The sword-carrying soldiers guard the Apostolic Palace and the gates of Vatican City and serve as bodyguards to the pope. Their official uniform is recognizable for its vivid stripes of Medici blue, red and yellow and its white collar and gloves.

A382: (d) German.

A383: (b) Switzerland. New recruits must also have attended a Swiss military school, must have a high school diploma or professional diploma, and must be between 19 and 30 years of age. Soldiers keep their posts for two to 25 years.

A384: (a) The Sack of Rome on May 6, 1527 by the troops of Charles V, Holy Roman Emperor, who turned Rome into a bloodbath. May 6 celebrates the bravery of the Swiss Guards on this day of bloodshed and death. After the Sack, 45,000 civilians were missing, some killed or wounded, others forced to flee. Although Charles V had sent his men to Rome, he had not intended for the troops to cause the massacre, which ensued after chaos broke out. The day kicked off eight days of looting and pillaging Catholic property and sacred sites, raping nuns, and slaughtering priests, monks and even orphans and hospital patients. The sacking is considered part of the War of the League of Cognac.

Q385: Which of the following is part of a major Easter tradition in France?
   a. Flying bells   d. Swimming bunnies
   b. Dancing fish   e. Colorful scarves
   c. Jumping jellybeans

Q386: Which is part of an Easter tradition in Bermuda?
   a. Javelin throwing   d. Somersaulting
   b. Spelunking   e. Fishing
   c. Kite flying

Q387: Which of the following is the only East Asian country that recognizes Christmas as a public holiday?
   a. Japan   d. China
   b. South Korea   e. Taiwan
   c. Mongolia

Q388: Name a major Christmas tradition in Mexico that involves a nine-day reenactment of Joseph's and Mary's searching for shelter just before Mary gave birth.
   a. Children's Day   d. Candlemas
   b. Holy Cross Day   e. Posadas
   c. Dance of the Flyers

Q389: In Mexico, the traditional date for children waking up to Christmas presents is not December 25. What is it?
   a. December 24   d. January 6
   b. March 25   e. December 8
   c. January 1

Q390: How do we figure out the date of Easter in a given year?
   a. First Sunday of April
   b. Last Sunday of March
   c. Sunday closest to first full moon in April
   d. Sunday closest to first crescent moon in April
   e. It's more complicated

A385: (a) Flying bells ("cloches volant" in French). In France, church bells stop ringing the day before Good Friday. Parents tell their children that the bells flew off to the Vatican in Rome with the grief of those mourning over Jesus' death. On Easter Sunday, the bells fly back to France dropping chocolate bells and chocolate eggs for children to find in their yards and gardens.

A386: (c) Kite flying. Bermudians fly colorful, hexagonal kites on Easter to symbolize Christ's ascent.

A387: (b) South Korea.

A388: (e) Posadas. This nine-day celebration leads up to Christmas and is celebrated by many Mexicans and Latin Americans.

A389: (d) January 6 (The Feast of the Epiphany). On the evening of January 5, children leave shoes by the door in hopes that the Three Wise Men will stuff them with gifts. The Feast of the Epiphany is also known as Three Kings Day or Little Christmas.

A390: (e) It's more complicated! Easter is celebrated on the first Sunday after the first full moon on or after the day of the vernal equinox, which is set at March 21 whether or not the equinox actually occurs on this day. No wonder most people just look at their calendars! Easter can never be before March 22 or after April 25.

Q391: Name the Catholic who was president of South Korea when he was awarded the 2000 Nobel Peace Prize.
>   a. Lee Myung-Bak
>   b. Roh Moo-Hyun
>   c. Kim Dae-jung
>   d. Kim Jong-un
>   e. Hu Kintao

Q392: What landmark surgery was Nobel Prize winner Joseph Murray first to perform on a human in 1954?
>   a. Lobotomy
>   b. Liposuction
>   c. Angioplasty
>   d. Appendectomy
>   e. Kidney transplant

Q393: Nobel Prize winner Sigrid Undset is considered one of the greatest Catholic _____ of the 20th century.
>   a. Pugilists
>   b. Novelists
>   c. Cartoonists
>   d. Metaphysicians
>   e. Dolphin trainers

Q394: Who is Agnes Goxha Bojaxhiu better known as?
>   a. Mother Teresa
>   b. Mother Angelica
>   c. Mother Cabrini
>   d. Mother Dolores Hart
>   e. Queen Isabella

A391: (c) Kim Dae-jung (1925-2009). He became Catholic in 1957, taking the baptismal name of Thomas More. Known for his Sunshine Policy of engagement with North Korea, Kim was the South Korean president from 1998 to 2003.

A392: (e) Human kidney transplant. Dr. Murray, a devout Catholic and American surgeon, won the Nobel Prize for Physiology or Medicine in 1990 for his work on organ and cell transplantation. He was appointed to the Pontifical Academy of Sciences in 1996 and is the author of *Surgery of the Soul: Reflections on a Curious Career* (2001).

A393: (b) Novelists. Sigrid Undset (1882-1949), a Norwegian novelist who became Catholic in 1924, won the Nobel Prize for Literature in 1928. Her best-known works are *Kristin Lavransdatter* and *Olav Audunsson*.

A394: (a) Mother Teresa (1910-1997). This 1979 winner of the Nobel Peace Prize was beatified by Pope John Paul II in 2003, receiving the title of Blessed Teresa of Calcutta. The devout Albanian nun founded the Missionaries of Charity in 1950 and spent the rest of her life serving the sick, dying and poorest of the poor in India and other countries.

Q395: "Catholicism is a deep matter – it cannot be taken up in a teacup."
    a. Allen Hunt   c. Pope Paul VI
    b. Perry Como   d. Fr. Frank Pavone
    e. Blessed John Henry Cardinal Newman

Q396: "There are not a hundred people in America who truly hate the Catholic Church. There are millions of people who hate what they wrongly believe to be the Catholic Church."
    a. Al Smith   d. Mother Teresa
    b. Mother Seton   e. President John F. Kennedy
    c. Archbishop Fulton J. Sheen

Q397: "Oh Lord, grant me chastity and continence, but not yet."
    a. Johann Eck   d. St. Augustine
    b. Peter Boyle   e. St. Patrick
    c. Gregory Peck

Q398: "In our time, the truth is often mistaken for the opinion of the majority."
    a. Gary Cooper   d. Liberace
    b. Pope John Paul II   e. Francis Ford Coppola
    c. Bill O'Reilly

Q399: "Ignorance of Scripture is ignorance of Christ."
    a. St. Jerome   d. St. Athanasius
    b. St. Paul   e. St. Cyril of Alexandria
    c. St. Peter

Q400: "For He carried that body in His hands."
    a. St. Jerome   d. St. Augustine
    b. St. Paul   e. St. John Chrysostom
    c. St. Peter

Q401: "The difficulty of explaining 'why I am Catholic' is that there are ten thousand reasons all amounting to one reason: that Catholicism is true."
    a. G.K. Chesterton   d. Samuel Alito
    b. Antonin Scalia   e. John G. Roberts
    c. Clarence Thomas

Q402: While speaking at Harvard University's Class Day 1982, which Catholic told the graduating seniors that on their wedding day, virginity would be "the greatest gift that the young man can give the young woman, and that the young woman can give the man"?
    a. Lorena Ochoa   d. Mother Teresa
    b. Phyllis Schlafly   e. Nicole Kidman
    c. Clare Boothe Luce

A395: (e) Blessed John Henry Cardinal Newman (in a February 1846 letter to an acquaintance, Spencer Northcote). The cardinal was beatified in 2010 by Pope Benedict XVI.

A396: (c) Archbishop Fulton J. Sheen. The quote is contained in the preface to *Radio Replies* by Frs. Leslie Rumble and Charles Carty. The book was originally published in 1938 and was re-published in 1979 by TAN Books in Rockford, Illinois.

A397: (d) St. Augustine (*Confessions* 8:7). Long before his conversion and baptism in the Catholic Church, St. Augustine would pray this prayer. Though still in his 13-year forbidden relationship with a concubine at the time, St. Augustine was gradually moving on a path to God.

A398: (b) Pope John Paul II (Homily of John Paul II for the Canonization of Edith Stein, October 11, 1998).

A399: (a) St. Jerome (*Commentary on Isaiah*, prologue).

A400: (d) St. Augustine. Referring to Jesus and the Last Supper, St. Augustine wrote: "Christ was carried in His own hands when, referring to His own body, He said, 'This is my body' [Mt 26:26]. For He carried that body in His hands" (*Explanations of the Psalms* 33:1:10 [405 A.D.]).

A401: (a) G.K. Chesterton, in his 1926 essay, "Why I Am a Catholic."

A402: (d) Mother Teresa. The text of the saint's talk is posted at www.columbia. edu/cu/augustine/arch/teresa82.html.

Q403: What was the first Catholic college in the United States?
a. Georgetown University
b. Notre Dame University
c. Boston College
d. Villanova University
e. Fordham University

Q404: Xavier University was the first Catholic college established for
_____ in the United States.
a. Latin Americans
b. African Americans
c. Asian Americans
d. Elderly students
e. Hearing impaired students

Q405: Name the only pope-chartered and bishop-sponsored university in
the United States.
a. John Paul the Great Catholic University
b. The Catholic University of America
c. University of Nebraska
d. Benedictine College
e. DeSales University

Q406: Which U.S. college campus features a giant mural of Jesus (known as
"Touchdown Jesus") on a library wall facing the football stadium?
a. Georgetown University
b. Notre Dame University
c. Boston College
d. Villanova University
e. Fordham University

Q407: Which of the following was not a graduate of Notre Dame University?
a. Joe Montana
b. Condoleeza Rice
c. Phil Donahue
d. Regis Philbin
e. Antonin Scalia

A403: (a) Georgetown University, Washington, D.C., founded in 1789.

A404: (b) African Americans. This New Orleans university dates back to 1915 when St. Katharine Drexel and the Sisters of the Blessed Sacrament established a high school. A College of Liberal Arts and Sciences was added in 1925, thus launching Xavier University.

A405: (b) The Catholic University of America in Washington, D.C. With the approval of Pope Leo XIII, the U.S. bishops founded the university in 1887. It continues to be the only national university of the Catholic Church in the United States.

A406: (b) University of Notre Dame, in Notre Dame, Indiana. Besides the mural, the campus features a magnificent gilded Golden Dome crowned by a statue of the Blessed Virgin that tops the college's main building, an ornate Basilica of the Sacred Heart, and an outdoor Lady of Lourdes Grotto. Notre Dame's football team has generated seven Heisman trophy winners.

A407: (e) U.S. Supreme Court Associate Justice Antonin Scalia is a graduate of Georgetown University.

Q408: What does the "N" in INRI stand for?
    a. Noel   d. Nuncio
    b. Nazarene   e. Nun
    c. Neophyte

Q409: What does "A.D." stand for?
    a. After Death   d. Apostolic Days
    b. Anno Domini   e. After Dinosaurs
    c. Après Dieu

Q410: "IHS" refers to the first three letters of _____ in Greek.
    a. "Genesis"   d. "Jerusalem"
    b. "Cross"   e. "Jesus"
    c. "Bible"

Q411: What does BVM stand for?
    a. A woman in the New Testament
    b. A man in the Old Testament
    c. A popular Catholic club
    d. A popular Catholic automobile
    e. A Catholic university

Q412: If your boyfriend's middle initials are "F.X.," his parents probably wanted to honor _____.
    a. A certain country
    b. A certain club
    c. A certain saint
    d. A certain president
    e. A certain Apostle

Q413: To what creature does the Greek word "Ichthys" refer?
    a. Fish   d. Pig
    b. Lamb   e. Scorpion
    c. Horse

Q414: Why do Jesuits have the initials "S.J." after their name?
    a. It stands for St. Joseph
    b. It stands for St. John
    c. It stands for Sacred Jerusalem
    d. It stands for Sons of Jerome
    e. It stands for Society of Jesus

A408: (b) Nazarene. INRI stands for "Jesus the Nazarene, King of the Jews" (*"Iesus Nazarenus Rex Iudaeorum"* in Latin). Pontius Pilate had the inscription put on Jesus' cross (Jn 19:19).

A409: (b) Anno Domini (Latin for "The Year of Our Lord"). B.C. stands for "Before Christ."

A410: (e) Jesus. "IHS" is the English transliteration of the first three letters of Jesus' name in Greek (ΙΗΣΟΥΣ or Ιησους). The transliteration is imperfect, as the Greek letter that looks like an upper-case H is actually an upper-case eta, or long e.

 A411: (a) The Blessed Virgin Mary.

A412: (c) St. Francis Xavier (1506-1552), one of the greatest missionaries in the history of the Church. Francis was a colleague of St. Ignatius of Loyola, who founded the Society of Jesus (the Jesuits).

A413: (a) Fish. This ancient symbol of Christianity, according to the original *Catholic Encyclopedia* (1909),* may have been chosen because of Jesus' miracle of the multiplication of the fish and loaves of bread. Also, the letters in the Greek word for fish serve as initials for the words of "Jesus Christ, Son of God, Savior" Ιησους Χριστος Θεου Υιος Σοτηρ [Iesous Christos Theou Huios Soter]).

A414: (e) S.J. stands for Society of Jesus, founded in the 16th century by St. Ignatius of Loyola. The Jesuits (www.jesuits.org) are today the largest religious order of the Church, numbering 20,000 priests and brothers around the world.

* www.newadvent.org/cathen/06083a.htm

Q415: What was Jesus' blood type?
    a. A
    b. B
    c. AB
    d. O positive
    e. O negative

Q416: During the 1917 apparitions of Mary in Fatima, Portugal, an angel appeared to the children seers. What word or phrase did the angel cry out three times?
    a. Penance
    b. Hail
    c. Holy
    d. Peace be with you
    e. Believe

Q417: Thanks to the visions of a mystic nun, what were searchers able to locate?
    a. Mary's house
    b. Mary's Bible
    c. Mary's sandals
    d. Joseph's table
    e. Joseph's tools

Q418: Maria Montessori, a devout Catholic from Italy who developed the Montessori Method of teaching, was the first female _____ in Italy.
    a. Principal
    b. Mayor
    c. Physician
    d. Engineer
    e. Linguist

A415: (c) If you guessed type AB that is our bet too! After all, blood of type AB was found on the Shroud of Turin, believed to be the cloth which covered Jesus' body in the tomb and which bears His image. Blood type AB was also detected on the Sudarium of Oviedo, a piece of cloth believed to have covered and cleaned Jesus' face. But there's more. Remember the Miracle of Lanciano in 711 A.D. where the bread and wine turned into visible flesh and blood during the Mass of a doubting priest? The flesh and blood from the miracle are preserved in a church in Italy. In the 1970s, the flesh was tested and determined to contain blood of type AB. Then, the pellets of blood were tested and came up as AB as well!

A416: (a) Penance! Penance! Penance!

A417: (a) Mary's house. A mystic nun's precise description helped investigators find the exact house in Turkey, outside Ephesus, where Mary was said to have lived into her old age with the Apostle St. John. The visionary was none other than Blessed Anne Catherine Emmerich (1774-1824).

A418: (c) Physician. The first female physician in Italy, Montessori (1870-1952) realized the need for new methods of education while treating disabled children. Today, her philosophy is implemented on six continents.

Q419: Where in Europe are the bodily remains of St. Peter?
  a. Vatican City
  b. Venice
  c. Madrid
  d. Jerusalem
  e. They disappeared

Q420: Where in Europe are the bodily remains of St. Paul?
  a. Malta
  b. Tarsus
  c. Damascus
  d. Rome
  e. Ephesus

Q421: Name the devout Catholic who became President of the European Council on December 1, 2009 after having been Prime Minister of Belgium.
  a. Herman Van Rompuy
  b. Boutros Boutros-Ghali
  c. Kofi Annan
  d. David Cameron
  e. Anders Fogh Rasmussen

Q422: Name the Catholic who led the Free French Forces in World War II, headed the provisional government after France's liberation, and served as president of France from 1959 to 1969.
  a. Charles de Gaulle
  b. Charles Martel
  c. Maréchal Tassigny
  d. Philippe Pétain
  e. Joseph Bonaparte

Q423: In 2009, the Vatican post office issued a stamp featuring a portrait of a famous Catholic who had been born 200 years earlier. Who was featured?
  a. David Livingstone
  b. Sacagawea
  c. Louis Braille
  d. Benito Juarez
  e. Rubén Salazar

A419: (a) Vatican City, beneath the high altar of St. Peter's Basilica. Peter was martyred under Emperor Nero during the first century persecution of Christians and was buried on the hill of the Vatican.

A420: (d) Rome. St. Paul's tomb was found in 2006 under the main altar of Rome's second largest basilica – Basilica of St. Paul Outside the Walls – by archeologist Giorgio Filippo and his team, according to the Vatican Press office. The basilica was founded by Emperor Constantine over St. Paul's tomb.

A421: (a) Herman Van Rompuy (b. 1947) was prime minister of Belgium for a year ending November 25, 2009. The author of six books on economics and politics, Van Rompuy reportedly made monthly retreats to the Affligem Abbey monastery.

A422: (a) Charles de Gaulle (1890-1970). General de Gaulle died holding a rosary that he had received from Pope Paul VI.

A423: (c) Louis Braille (1809-1852), the French inventor of the revolutionary Braille system of writing and reading for the blind. Also in 2009, the United States issued a commemorative coin honoring Braille. The coin features his portrait and raised dots spelling "Brl" in Braille.

Q424: What strange occurrence was seen in the sky in 1917 by 70,000 or more people in Portugal?
    a. Darkness at noon
    b. Luminous doves
    c. Visible corona
    d. Simultaneous lunar and solar eclipse
    e. The sun danced

Q425: Which of the following was built as a bell tower for a cathedral?
    a. Leaning Tower of Pisa
    b. Eiffel Tower
    c. Big Ben
    d. Taj Mahal
    e. Tower of London

Q426: According to a long-standing Christian tradition, which of the Twelve Apostles is buried in Spain?
    a. St. Philip
    b. St. Andrew
    c. St. Jude
    d. St. James the Lesser
    e. St. James the Greater

Q427: Which island nation in the Mediterranean Sea hosts a major celebration every February 10 to celebrate the Apostle St. Paul's shipwreck on its land?
    a. Crete
    b. Sicily
    c. Mallorca
    d. Majorca
    e. Malta

A424: (e) The sun danced and zigzagged in the sky, then suddenly dropped toward earth only to rise again. The Miracle of the Sun was seen by thousands of people in Fatima, Portugal who had shown up that day – October 13, 1917 – because the Blessed Mother had promised three children that she would perform a miracle on that day for everyone to see. For more information, do an Internet search for "Miracle of the Sun" and "Fatima."

A425: (a) Leaning Tower of Pisa. Next to the tower is the magnificent Pisa Cathedral – a masterpiece of Romanesque architecture – whose construction began in 1093.

A426: (e) St. James the Greater is said to be buried in Santiago de Compostela, Spain. In 813 A.D., a supernatural event led to the discovery and identification of the Apostle's tomb. The tomb is a popular pilgrimage site today. St. James is the patron saint of Spain.

A427: (e) Malta. Today, 94 percent of Malta's population is Catholic. While shipwrecked for three months, St. Paul preached Christianity and performed miracles. Many Maltese regard St. Paul's shipwreck in 60 A.D. as the best thing that ever happened to their country. The shipwreck is described in the Acts of the Apostles (27:13 to 28:16).

Q428: Known as the Father of Monasticism, St. Anthony of Egypt was not the first monk, but he was one of the first monks to do what?
   a. Make a vow of silence
   b. Live alone in the desert
   c. Fast for 40 days
   d. Translate the Bible
   e. Eat meat

Q429: Where did the Desert Fathers live?
   a. Scetes desert in Egypt
   b. Sahara desert in Morocco
   c. Gobi desert in Mongolia
   d. Antarctic desert in Antarctica
   e. Pumas desert in Spain

Q430: Name the hermit who lived in a cave in an Egyptian desert from age 16 until the age of 113.
   a. St. John of God
   b. St. Paul the Hermit
   c. St. Gregory the Illuminator
   d. St. Mary of Egypt
   e. St. Sarah of the Desert

Q431: Which of the following is not typical of a monk's life in a cloistered monastery?
   a. Prayer, fasting, penance, and daily Mass
   b. Poverty
   c. Manual labor
   d. Visiting Third World countries
   e. Permanent residence in one monastery

Q432: Which brand of champagne was named after a Benedictine monk?
   a. Dom Perignon
   b. Krug
   c. Cristal
   d. Laurent Perrier
   e. Bollinger

A428: (b) He was committed to living in the desert, completely cut off from civilization. St. Anthony of Egypt (251-356 A.D.) remained in the rugged Western Desert west of the Nile for 13 years.

A429: (a) Scetes (or "Nitrian") desert in Egypt. The Desert Fathers were the Christian hermits, ascetics and monks who, beginning in the 3rd century, lived in solitude in Scetes.

A430: (b) St. Paul the Hermit (also known as St. Paul of Thebes). St. Paul the Hermit's hollowed out cave from the third and fourth century can be visited today on the grounds of the Monastery of St. Paul in Egypt. Read more about him in St. Jerome's work, "The Life of Paulus the First Hermit," written during his own residence in the desert of Syria in 374 or 375 A.D.

A431: (d) Visiting Third World countries. Cloistered monks are rarely allowed to leave the monastery. The Carmelite Monks of Wyoming (www.carmelitemonks. org), for example, live solitary lives in a monastery under the Rocky Mountains, toiling away at agrarian chores, daily sacrifices and prayers for the purification of the whole Church. Though they do not make a vow of silence, they may only speak during one hour of the day.

A432: (a) Dom Perignon. The prestigious champagne consists of 55 percent Chardonnay and 45 percent Pinot Noir. The French monk known as Dom Perignon (c. 1638-1715) is credited with advances in sparkling wine production methods. Back then, monks commonly tended to church vineyards to produce wine for Mass.

Q433: Who coined the famous phrase, "A family that prays together stays together"?
  a. A man known as the Rosary Priest d. Billy Graham
  b. A woman known as the Crying Nun e. Mother Angelica
  c. A boy known as the Pious Pizza Boy

Q434: The ancient saying, "When in Rome, do as the Romans do," originally referred to:
  a. Local fasting customs d. Ancient Italian spaghetti sauce
  b. Early Christian toga fashions e. The Olympics
  c. Kissing the pope's ring

Q435: Leonardo da Vinci's oil painting, The *Virgin and Child with St. Anne,* depicts the baby Jesus with his mother and maternal grandmother, St. Anne. In the painting, what animal is the baby Jesus playing with?
  a. Puppy d. Lamb
  b. Kitten e. Owl
  c. Pony

Q436: The title of a mural by Michelangelo (lost, but preserved in an engraving) consists of the names of four consecutive ancestors of Jesus. What is the fourth name in the title? *Abraham, Isaac, Jacob, _____.*
  a. Judah d. Jehoshaphat
  b. Joseph e. Jogue
  c. Jared

Q437: Which of the following is *not* one of the children of a famous comic strip family created by a Philadelphia-born Catholic cartoonist in 1960? (Hint: The comic strip is still running.)
  a. Billy d. Cookie
  b. Dolly e. P.J.
  c. Jeffy

Q438: Mother Dolores Hart, who has been a cloistered Benedictine nun in Connecticut for 50 years, has the distinction of being the first girl to _____.
  a. Convince Henri Matisse to design a chapel
  b. Pose for Picasso
  c. Kiss Elvis on the big screen
  d. Star in *The Sound of Music*
  e. Fly an airplane

A433: (a) The coiner of the phrase, Fr. Patrick Peyton, C.S.C. (1909-1992), was dubbed "the Rosary Priest" because of his crusade to spread rosary devotion after his prayer request to the Blessed Mother to recover from incurable tuberculosis was granted. The Irish-born priest founded Family Theater Productions, a radio and film venture, formerly on Hollywood Boulevard in Hollywood, California, which featured hundreds of famous stars, including James Dean, Ronald Reagan, James Cagney, and Bob Hope. The venture currently operates from Sunset Boulevard in Hollywood.

A434: (a) In the late 4th century, St. Augustine's mother, St. Monica, was troubled to find that although Christians in Rome were fasting on Saturdays, Christians in Milan were not. St. Augustine wrote to his mentor, St. Ambrose, who was bishop of Milan, for advice. St. Ambrose responded, "When I am here I do not fast on Saturday; but when I am at Rome I do: whatever church you may come to, conform to its custom." The bishop's advice was later rephrased to the pithier quote in the question. The original quote can be found in St. Augustine's Letter 36 (14:32), written in 396 A.D.

A435: (d) Lamb (interpreted as a sacrificial lamb representing Christ's Passion).

A436: (a) Judah.

A437: (d) Cookie is not. Billy (7), Dolly (5), and Jeffy (3), and their baby sibling, P.J. are the fictional children who have appeared in the comic strip *The Family Circus* for more than 50 years. Created by Philadelphia-born Bil Keane (1922-2011), the single-panel cartoon appears in about 1,500 newspapers today. Today, Keane's real son, Jeff, writes, inks and colors the comic strip. The elder Keane once illustrated a book by his friend and fellow Catholic, humorist Erma Bombeck.

A438: (c) Kiss Elvis on the big screen. The beautiful Dolores Hart, born Dolores Hicks in 1938, had co-starring roles in Elvis movies such as *Loving You* (1957) and *King Creole* (1958). She entered a monastery in Bethlehem, Connecticut in 1963 and has stated in interviews that she is now with the One she loves. Today, she is an Oscar-voting member of the Academy of Motion Picture Arts and Sciences. Hart was the subject of a 2012 Oscar-nominated HBO short documentary *God is Bigger than Elvis*.

Q439: Who was the author of *The Defense of the Seven Sacraments* (1521)?
　　a. Martin Luther
　　b. St. Thomas Aquinas
　　c. Pope Leo X
　　d. King Henry VIII
　　e. St. Bonaventure

Q440: Name the first century figure who is the subject of the famous 1959 novel, *Dear and Glorious Physician.*
　　a. St. Luke
　　b. St. Joseph
　　c. Jesus
　　d. St. Augustine
　　e. St. Jerome

Q441: Sister Maria Celeste and the letters she wrote to her famous father in the early 1600s were the subject of a 1999 book entitled _____.
　　a. *Copernicus' Daughter*
　　b. *Galileo's Daughter*
　　c. *Newton's Daughter*
　　d. *Kepler's Daughter*
　　e. *Archimedes' Daughter*

A439: (d) King Henry VIII of England (1491-1547). He wrote the work as a refutation of Martin Luther's *The Babylonian Captivity of the Church*. The book was dedicated to Pope Leo X and was written before the Church of England broke away from the Catholic Church.

A440: (a) St. Luke, the third Gospel writer. St. Paul refers to St. Luke as "the beloved physician" (Col 4:14). The novel was written by Taylor Caldwell.

A441: (b) *Galileo's Daughter* by Dava Sobel. Italian astronomer Galileo Galilei (1564-1642) and Marina Gamba had a son and two daughters, both of whom entered the convent of San Matteo in 1614 near Florence, Italy. Galileo's oldest daughter, Virginia, upon taking the vows of a nun, took the name "Sister Maria Celeste." The name "Celeste" was chosen to honor her father and his studies of the heavens.

Q442: The first time that a Mexican president attended a papal Mass was July 31, 2002. What occasion did the Mass celebrate?
 a. Ground-breaking for new cathedral
 b. Overthrow of dictator Porfirio Diaz
 c. Anniversary of Montezuma's death
 d. Constitutional amendment to restore religious freedom
 e. Canonization of St. Juan Diego

Q443: Name the largest city in South America. (Hint: It was named after an Apostle who wrote almost half of the books of the New Testament.)
 a. San Juan
 b. Santiago
 c. San José
 d. San Antonio
 e. São Paulo

Q444: Name the South American country whose capital was named after one of the original Twelve Apostles.
 a. Chile
 b. Uruguay
 c. Paraguay
 d. Bolivia
 e. Venezuela

Q445: Name the South American country whose capital was named for a doctrine concerning the Virgin Mary.
 a. Peru
 b. Chile
 c. Paraguay
 d. Bolivia
 e. Venezuela

Q446: Name the South American country that was named after a Catholic explorer.
 a. Peru
 b. Brazil
 c. Ecuador
 d. Colombia
 e. Argentina

Q447: What is the highest capital city in the world?
 a. Lima, Peru
 b. La Paz, Bolivia
 c. Buenos Aires, Argentina
 d. Brasília, Brazil
 e. Bogotá, Colombia

Q448: After whom was it named?
 a. Sancho Panza
 b. Simón Bolívar
 c. José de San Martín
 d. The Virgin Mary
 e. St. Rose of Lima

A442: (e) The canonization Mass of St. Juan Diego (1474-1548) was attended by President Vincente Fox. The 16th century apparitions of the Lady of Guadalupe to this saint helped spread the Catholic faith in Mexico. The Church does not require the faithful to believe in private apparitions such as these.

A443: (e) São Paulo, Brazil, with a population of about 11 million, was named after the Apostle, St. Paul. The original village was founded by two Jesuit missionary priests on January 25, 1554 with a celebratory Mass. The chosen date commemorated the day of St. Paul's dramatic conversion.

A444: (a) Chile, whose capital, Santiago, refers to the Apostle known as St. James the Greater. In Spanish, St. James is known as "San Jacobo" or "Santiago El Mayor." "San" means "saint," while "Iago" is short for "Iacobus," which is Jacob in Latin. Other cities named after St. James include Santiago de Cuba (the most important city in Cuba after Havana) and Santiago de Compostela in Spain.

A445: (c) Paraguay, whose capital, Asunción, was named after the Assumption of the Blessed Virgin Mary – an event whereby God brought or assumed Mary's body and soul into heaven. Asunción got its start when Juan de Salazar founded a fort in 1537 and named it Nuestra Señora de la Asunción ("Our Lady of the Assumption"). The fort became a city in 1541, making Asunción one of the oldest cities in South America.

A446: (d) Colombia. Other places named after Christopher Columbus include the District of Columbia (Washington, D.C.), Columbus, Ohio, and Columbia, South Carolina.

A447: (b) La Paz, Bolivia, located in the Andes mountains.

A448: (d) The Virgin Mary, under her title, "Our Lady of Peace." In fact, the official name of Bolivia's capital is La Señora de la Paz.

Q449: Name the Central American country whose capital was named after a male New Testament saint.
    a. Panama   d. Honduras
    b. Costa Rica   e. Guatemala
    c. El Salvador

Q450: After whom was Puerto Rico's capital – San Juan – named?
    a. St. John the Apostle   d. St. Joan of Arc
    b. St. John the Baptist   e. King John of England
    c. St. John Bosco (Don Bosco)

Q451: Name the oldest European-founded city in the New World. (Hint: It was named after the founder of the Friars Preachers).
    a. Baton Rouge   d. San José
    b. St. Augustine   e. Havana
    c. Santo Domingo

Q452: When Secretary of State Hillary Clinton saw the life-size image of the Blessed Virgin Mary at the Basilica of Guadalupe in Mexico on March 26, 2009, what did she say?
    a. "Breathtaking"   d. "Who painted it?"
    b. "A true masterpiece"   e. She said nothing
    c. "It truly looks like Mary"

Q453: Name the devout Catholic who became the first woman president of any nation in Central America.
    a. Violeta Chamorro   d. Michelle Bachelet Jeria
    b. Isabel Perón   e. Cristina Fernández de Kirchner
    c. Laura Chinchilla Miranda

Q454: Named after a South American saint, which California city is the largest city in California Wine Country?
    a. Santa Ana   d. Santa Monica
    b. Santa Barbara   e. Santa Rosa
    c. Santa Clara

Q455: In 1889, Pope Leo XIII awarded the Golden Rose to a princess for her role in abolishing slavery in her South American country. Which country was it?
    a. Peru   d. Colombia
    b. Brazil   e. Argentina
    c. Ecuador

A449: (b) Costa Rica, whose capital, San José (St. Joseph), was founded in 1738.

A450: (b) St. John the Baptist ("San Juan Bautista" in Spanish).

A451: (c) Santo Domingo, capital of the Dominican Republic. The city and country were named after St. Dominic (1170-1221), founder of the Catholic religious order known as the Friars Preachers or the "Dominicans." Santo Domingo was founded in 1496 by Bartholomew Columbus, brother of Christopher Columbus, and was the first seat of Spanish colonial rule in the New World.

A452: (d) "Who painted it?" The answer was "God!" as Monsignor Diego Monroy, rector of the basilica, replied. The image was miraculously imprinted on St. Juan Diego's cloak (or "tilma") in 1531, and has remained freshly colored and structurally intact for almost 600 years, even surviving a bombing and contact with acid. The tilma has been studied by scientists ranging from a chemistry Nobel Prize winner to a professor from NASA.

A453: (a) Violeta Chamorro. Born in 1929, Chamorro served as president of Nicaragua from 1990 to 1997 after defeating incumbent Daniel Ortega, head of the Sandinistas, in the 1990 elections. Chamorro worked for peace, democracy, and economic stability.

A454: (e) Santa Rosa, named after St. Rose of Lima.

A455: (b) Brazil. The recipient of the papal honor was Isabel I (1846-1921), Princess Imperial, who signed the Golden Law in 1888, abolishing slavery in the Brazilian Empire. Her nickname was "Isabel the Redeemer." Her father, Pedro II (1825-1891), was the second and last emperor of Brazil, having ruled for 58 years. Today, popes usually award the Golden Rose to shrines and basilicas rather than to people.

Q456: Which Spanish-speaking country was named after God?
a. Peru
b. Chile
c. Paraguay
d. Bolivia
e. El Salvador

Q457: What gift did Peru's former president, Alan Garcia, give his country just before leaving office in 2011?
a. A diocesan seminary
b. A religious museum
c. A giant statue of Christ
d. A Michelangelo painting
e. Ancient Incan documents

A456: (e) El Salvador. It means "The Savior."

A457: (c) A giant statue of Christ called Christ of the Pacific. The 120-foot structure overlooks Lima's bay and beaches. Garcia said he wanted a figure that "blesses Peru and protects Lima." The statue ranks as one of the tallest Christ statues in the world, along with famous ones in Swiebodzin, Poland (2010), Manado City, Indonesia (2007) and ones in Rio de Janeiro, Brazil (1931) and Cochabamba, Bolivia (1994).

Q458: Which is not true about Avery Dulles (1918-2008), the renowned American theologian who was appointed to the College of Cardinals by Pope John Paul II in 2001?
- a. His father, great-grandfather, and great-uncle served as U.S. Secretary of State
- b. His uncle headed the C.I.A.
- c. He never served as bishop
- d. In 1940, he graduated from Harvard and became Catholic
- e. An experience along the Mississippi River caused him to believe in God

Q459: Which Catholic sitcom star told Catholic News Service in 2012 that his faith was growing constantly and he wanted to do projects that would "glorify God in every way"?
- a. Ray Romano (*Everybody Loves Raymond*)
- b. Kevin James (*King of Queens*)
- c. Johnny Galecki (*Big Bang Theory*)
- d. Steve Carell (*The Office*)
- e. Tony Shalhoub (*Monk*)

Q460: Attorney Nellie Gray (1924-2012), a convert to Catholicism, founded one of the largest annual peaceful marches in Washington, D.C. Name the march.
- a. Occupy Wall Street
- b. Million Man March
- c. March for Life
- d. Appalachia Rising
- e. October Rebellion

Q461: Which of the following athletes was not a practicing Catholic?
- a. Pelé, Brazil's most famous soccer player
- b. Bobby Allison, NASCAR Hall of Famer
- c. Babe Ruth, legendary baseball player
- d. Jim Thorpe, one of the greatest athletes of all time
- e. Tim Tebow, NFL quarterback

A458: (e) It was an experience along the Charles River that caused Dulles – who would later become a Jesuit priest – to believe in God while he was a Harvard student. Although he was raised a Presbyterian, he considered himself agnostic when he entered Harvard. His observation of a tree starting to blossom caused him to believe that God existed. His father, John Foster Dulles, served as Secretary of State under President Dwight Eisenhower and his uncle, Allen Dulles, directed the Central Intelligence Agency.

A459: (b) Kevin James starred as Doug Heffernan on the sitcom *King of Queens* and co-starred in comedic movies such as *Here Comes the Boom*, *Zookeeper* and *Grown Ups*. Born Kevin Knipfing, the actor said that watching the movie *The Passion of the Christ* compelled him to enter more deeply into his faith.

A460: (c) March for Life. Gray started the event in 1974 to protest the 1973 Supreme Court decision of Roe vs. Wade.

A461: (e) Tim Tebow. Though not Catholic, Tebow is a devout Christian who created the now-famous "Tebowing" pose. "Tebowing" means getting down on one knee and praying, something the New York Jets quarterback is famous for doing before games.